To Jim a f...
Veteran
Chriest John T. ...

VIETNAM
curse or blessing

VIETNAM
curse or blessing

by
John L. Steer
with
Cliff Dudley

New Leaf Press

P.O. BOX 311, GREEN FOREST, AR 72638

First Edition, 1982

Photo Cover: Broken Lens Studio
Harrison, Arkansas

First Printing, 1982
Second Printing, 1984
Third Printing, 1987

Typesetting by Type-O-Graphics
Springfield, MO 65806

Library of Congress Catalog Number: 82-082016
International Standard Book Number: 0-89221-091-5

DEDICATION

I want to dedicate this book to:

- —the families of those 58,000 brave men who selflessly served and gave their lives for the principles of freedom on which this country was founded.
- —those about 2½ million dutiful men who continue to wear the scars and memories in their bodies and souls.
- —the families and to those that served. May you find everlasting peace in Jesus Christ.

My prayer is that when our country is again confronted with war we will stand, one nation under God, undivided.

Contents

Dedication
Publisher's Foreword
Chapter 1   Trying to Survive 11
Chapter 2   "Mr. Tough Guy" 21
Chapter 3   Airborne Infantry 41
Chapter 4   Jump School 63
Chapter 5   Vietnam 77
Chapter 6   Dak To 103
Chapter 7   Hill 875 111
Chapter 8   Being Put Back Together 125
Chapter 9   Back to the States 136
Chapter 10   Donna 149
Chapter 11   The Way Out 156
Chapter 12   Adding Wisdom to Zeal 174
Chapter 13   Curse or Blessing? 188

PUBLISHER'S FOREWORD

Vietnam was the war that almost everyone in America has tried to forget. For the first time in the history of the United States, America fought a war that it did not win. There were riots in the streets and on the college campuses, marchers and dissentients shouting obscenities to politicians who could not bring the war to an end. To add to our shame, students were killed by our National Guard at Kent State. To silence the cries of our veterans has been impossible, they and those who gave sons and husbands for the cause want to have recognition and honor instead of shame and disgrace.

New Leaf Press brings to you this heart-rending story of one man's defeat and victory. John Steer's life struggle to find peace and happiness will bring hope and blessings to veterans that have fought in wars.

John arrived in Vietnam hardly eighteen years old. Full of hate and violence, he was ready to kill the enemy. Several months later John came home with his right arm missing, a leg barely usable, and wounds virtually covering every part of his body. Steer was a physical and mental wreck yet with determination to overcome every obstacle. Full of revenge during the daytime, and terrible and appalling nightmares at night, his mind cracked. Seemingly his only answer was four years of psychiatric care.

Moving to the hills of northwest Arkansas, John discovered a man whose name is Jesus, who became his Saviour, and his Great Physician. Through Him he found the peace, the forgiveness, the purpose and the victory for which he had so long sought.

—The Publisher

1
TRYING TO SURVIVE

"Mom," I shouted, startling myself somewhat as my voice broke the eerie silence that prevailed in our one-room house, "Where's my daddy and when is he coming home?"

"John, that is the fourth time you have asked me that question today," Mom replied. "Your daddy's a Mess Sergeant in the army in a land called Japan. I hope that he will be home very soon. Now please be quiet and let me finish supper."

and squashed my nose tight against the frost-covered windowpane. The snow continued to fall, making everything in sight a white fairy land. Suddenly the wind started blowing and howling through the tall unbending Minnesota pines. *The thick quilt will feel good over me tonight, this is going to be a cold one. I sure wish my daddy was here,* I thought.

Winters in Minnesota were bitter cold and long, but we somehow managed to survive until spring. The cold was so cold that Mom added salt to the rinse water so she could hang the clothes out to dry and they wouldn't freeze stiff.

When Dad finally came home from Japan he had a buddy with him. I was terrified of them and hid behind the bed. In a one-room house that wasn't much hiding. They laughed and joked and seemed to ignore me. As the days passed I got to know Dad somewhat, but my fear of him stayed with me. Dad worked very hard and long hours on the railroad. It appeared to me all of my parents' time was consumed with trying to survive day by day.

Most of my early remembrance of my life is hate, rejection and confusion. Perhaps what I remember far exceeds reality, but my bitterness seemed to begin at birth and plagued me for over twenty-five years.

Being with my dad was great. One time he took me, with a bunch of other men, and shot several bears. The poor creatures didn't have a chance—the men waited at the town dump and when the bears came to eat they simply picked them off one at a time. It was a sad and glad experience.

As a youth I was not only very rebellious but adventurous. I was always going into the woods; much too far for a youngster. For protection I would drag along an old tomato basket—it was small on the bottom and big on the top. If anything tries to get me, I'll hide under the basket, I reasoned. One time my parents and a few of the neighbors came looking for me. They were worried that I was really lost.

I wasn't lost, only hiding and they soon found me. What a brat I must have been. Once in total desperation Mom tied me to the clothes line to keep me from running away. When Dad saw there were wolf tracks around the area, Mom gave up on that idea.

There was a time my dad made me a bow and arrow at work. It must have taken a lot of time and effort, and I really appreciated it but never told him. As I got a little older, sometimes Dad would take me to work with him. I'd throw the transformer switches for him at the railroad. I thought I was the smartest kid on earth, but for some strange reason I never felt close to my dad.

Simple things made me happy, like a box of Kellogg's Corn Flakes with the mask on the back. My little brother and I would cut them out, tie a string around them and wear them on our faces. We never seemed to frighten anyone, but we had fun.

Mom was always trying to get me to take a nap. I'd joke with her and say, "A minute nap?" Finally she'd say, "Okay." Well, a minute nap was me running and jumping on the bed, lying there for a few seconds, jumping up, and that was my nap for the day.

My folks were really poor. Grandmother would sometimes bring a couple of bags of groceries, and also buy things for my brother and me. My aunt and her husband were a little better off financially. They lived quite a way off, but they'd come once in a while and bring us something. One time they brought my little brother and I bicycles. Boy, that was really a big deal for us! I didn't think there was enough money in the world for us to have something like bicycles. The world took on new meaning as we raced around on those beautiful machines.

We moved from the country life of Anoka to the slums of South Minneapolis. It seemed from there everything was downhill for the next twenty years of my life.

Dad bought a grocery store in the slums. He dealt with mostly low-class people. Drinking had been a family problem, but now it seemed to escalate. It started affecting my folk's marriage, my father's and my relationship, and I went deeper into myself—full of hate and rebellion. Frustration took over.

Dad tried to be buddies with me, but nothing worked. I was afraid to receive or give love. In the midst of all the tenements, apartment buildings, Dad took the time out to make me a big teepee. He sewed pieces of canvas together and really made an authentic one. I was happy for a day or two, but it was like nothing satisfied me. No matter what Dad did for me I couldn't show my appreciation.

Everything seemed to go wrong. Simple things became catastrophes to me. Like the time Mom was handing me a quart of tomatoes from the cupboard and it slipped out of her hand and fell on my head. I was taken to the hospital and was given a special little cap because I had suffered a skull fracture.

Again, I was riding my tricycle and bumped against a ledge and cut up my arm. That time it wasn't a hospital trip. Dad decided he could fix it up himself. He took some tape and made several butterfly stitches. I still have the scar to this day.

At the age of eight I was becoming pretty mouthy. I started talking back to my parents; yet I was still terrified of my father. One day Dad asked, "John, you really would like it if I'd move away and didn't live here, wouldn't you?"

He seemed to be in a good humor when he asked the question so I felt real brave and said, "Yeah, Dad, I guess I would rather that you didn't live here." I thought he was making a joke of it, and that was my chance to agree with him, and believe it or not, he left.

He was gone that time for a couple of days. When he returned he used me as his excuse for being gone. Let me tell you, my mother came in and just tore me up from one side to the other with her mouth because I had run Dad off.

Several weeks later Dad came into my bedroom. He began to curse at me. I'm certainly feeling very insecure. I hadn't done anything. I was too little to do anything serious. He had been drinking and apparently he and mother had been having a row.

"You need some air in here," he yelled as he punched out the windows with his fist. He wheeled around and left. For hours I laid there afraid to move, wondering what was coming next.

The grocery store seemed to be an albatross around the family's neck. One day a man from the neighborhood backed my mother into the cooler with a switchblade and tried to molest her. Dad happened to come into the store about that time and pulled a gun on the man. He told him to get out and better never come back. He then put him in the car and kicked a dent in his car door.

The man was taken to court, but nothing ever happened. I remember as child my father saying over and over the police told him that he should have shot him in the leg or something because nothing would happen in the courts. They simply put a restraining order against him to stay away from the store.

From that event it seemed I was always afraid that somebody was going to hurt my mother. Gypsies would come into the store and take a bite out of an apple and say, "How much do you want for this? This apple has a bite out of it." Everyone seemed to be stealing us blind.

Most of the kids that I played with in the neighborhood were two or three years older than me. As a result, at an early age I learned a lot out of the gutter. Most of these poor children had been involved in rape, incest, immorality, stealing, booze and drugs. I learned quick that it was the survival of the fittest.

The girls in the neighborhood were extra tough. They were always trying to get us boys to go to bed with them. It made me feel proud because I was looking for security, friendship, and for someone to love. I was a candidate for anything that goes.

The store continued to go downhill. Dad would come in and take out some money from the till. There were some times that Mom wouldn't have money to make change. His drinking also seemed to be getting the best of him.

To add to all their problems, one afternoon I was carving on an old wooden box with all my might when it slipped, and I pretty near cut off my finger with a double-edge razor blade. Mom rushed me to the hospital. She had to sign special papers because at that time it was an experiment to try and sew a finger back on. The doctors peeled it down both sides so they could sew the leaders, tendons and nerves together. For several months I had to go to the doctor every day. I'd take a cab to downtown Minneapolis and get a penicillin shot. I loved it! I didn't like the shot, but Mom would always give me enough money to buy a hot fudge sundae. I thought I was really a big shot. I was on my own! Mom didn't go with me as she had to work in the store.

I had a job at the store, too, sorting bottles. The whole basement was a mess of bottles, and I tried to keep it straight.

Things got so bad that we lost the store and moved to New Brighton. The move wasn't far, only about thirty miles. We lived there with my grandmother.

Even though I was in third grade at New Brighton, the teacher soon discovered I couldn't read. Dad didn't know about it. He apparently had not kept up with my schooling and grades. Now, all of a sudden, they're going to put me back a grade.

Dad went into a rage. He sat me down, put a book in front of me and said, "Read this!"

I couldn't read it.

He hit me and screamed, "Now, read this!"

Again I couldn't read it.

He hit me again, and screamed at me: "Now read this!"

I couldn't. I was shaking violently, and the more I shook, the more he hit me and screamed. I didn't think it was ever going to end, but finally it did.

They did, however, put me back a grade and that was real hard on my ego. I lied and told everyone I wanted to be put back so I could be in the same grade with my girl friend.

That was also the year my dad gave me a 22-rifle. Then I really felt my oats. However, it was over two years before I was allowed to shoot it.

Everything in my life was one disappointment after another. Even mother nature seemed to be against me. I found some baby squirrels and brought them down out of the tree. I had my shirt filled with squirrels! My mother liked to have had a heart attack. She told me to take them back to the nest at once. As I approached the tree, the mother squirrel tried to eat me up. She was jumping all over me. I guess that was to be my fate in life.

Grandma's house was really a business complex. The living quarters were above a grocery store, butcher shop, bakery, and a Ford garage.

I worked in the butcher shop, swept the floor, washed the butcher counter, and put sawdust on the floor every day. The butcher paid me 50 cents a week, plus he'd always give me beef for fishing. He'd give me really good beef. In other words, he was helping feed our family, and he knew it. I would take the beef upstairs, and Mom would cut off all the good beef and I would get the suet, which was all I needed for fishing. In disguise, the butcher was a saint, of sorts, in giving us a helping hand. I also worked from time to time for the bakery—helping clean up. We'd get free donuts thrown in as a part of the salary.

My Uncle Jim had gone into the Air Force just before we moved in with Grandma. I couldn't resist the temptation of all the stuff in his closet. I'd sneak the BB-gun and pistols outside and play with them. I got the BB-gun outside one day, and shot my brother in the stomach. We were playing cowboy and Indians, and I got carried away. He started crying and screaming.

I said, "Please don't tell Mama. Please don't tell. Here, shoot me." I loaded the gun and gave it to him. He shot me right through the lip, but he didn't squeal on me.

There was a creek a couple of blocks from our house, and it became my favorite spot. One time coming back from the creek, a lizard ran up my pants leg and bit me and wouldn't turn loose. I stood in the middle of the road screaming for help. The cars stopped and lined up behind me. A lady came running toward me, and I screamed, "There's something biting me!" She pulled down my pants in the middle of the road (with all those cars lined up!) and took that lizard off of me and threw it in the ditch. Believe it or not, I was too scared to be embarrassed.

Another time by the creek, I found a big paper hornets' nest. These were the big, long orange and black hornets—the kind that attack you. I knocked down the nest—nothing! I had a plastic bag with me, so I put the hornet's nest in the bag. As soon as I started home I saw a big hornet flying around inside the bag. There was a hole in the bag so I had to twist it with one hand, and hold it with the other hand. The nest was full of hornets, and I didn't know it. I took the nest home to show to Mother and Aunt Edith. They both started screaming, "Get that thing out of here. We will all be stung to death."

By then, there were about 200 of these things flying around inside the plastic bag, and I didn't know what to do with it. I suddenly knew that I had a time bomb in my grip! I ran downstairs to the garage. One of the men told me to submerge it in the used-oil barrel. Before it came to the top he lit the oil, and that took care of a near natural disaster.

2
"MR. TOUGH GUY"

We soon moved back to Minneapolis. The twenty-apartment complex building looked like an old castle. We were only five blocks from the real slums, but believe me, the same type people lived in our apartment house. There were dopers, pimps, whores, alcoholics, and anything else you want to put on the list.

It was here that I learned the real art of stealing. I'd pay someone else to do it for me. There were several Indians in the apartment so I hired one of them to do my dirty work. I'd give him a few firecrackers, and he would steal the bike. Then I could tell my folks: "I bought it."

To survive I soon learned the law of the "city jungle." The toughest and strongest wins; the weakest gets beat up! I read every book on the martial arts I could get my hands on. Soon I was breaking boards with my fists. I would throw knives, and then throw knives again. I got in trouble for ruining the side of the garage and every tree in sight, but I was known for being fast with a knife.

With all of the hate and violence surrounding me I became very hardened emotionally. As a result, my relationship with Dad got worse and worse. Slowly I began to hate him. I feared him more now than ever. I dreamed about killing him. I used to pray to God all the time: *God, kill my father. You know how rotten he is. You know what he's done to Mother. You know what he's done to me. Kill him, God, kill him!* I don't know how many times I prayed that prayer. I don't think I felt too guilty about it either. I used to pray that God could kill him in such a way that Mother wouldn't feel too bad—like an accident. Satan was controlling me and I didn't even realize it.

Everytime Mother threatened to leave—which was many times—I would tell her, "Please don't go back to him this time, Mom, please stay away. Don't go back to him. Please don't go back to him." Eventually she'd always go back to him.

One time their fight became real violent, and I feared for her life. We went to the park afterwards. Mom and I were both crying. She was sitting on a park bench. I screamed, "Mom, we can make it without Dad. We don't need him. Please, this time, don't go back to him. Please don't go back to him."

She promised that she wouldn't.

We came home from the park and I told my little brother, "If Dad ever touches my mother again I'm going to kill him."

Jerry told Dad right away what I had said. He

called me in and said, "Did you say" (he cursed me) "that you'd kill me if I ever touched your mother again?"

I looked him right in the eye and said, "Yes, sir, I did."

Mother used to scream at me and say that I had the eyes of the devil. She would hit me, and I would lay on the floor, or wherever I ended up, glaring at her. I'd never take my eyes off of her. The more she would hit me, the more hateful I would become. I wouldn't cry, I'd simply look at her. (I'm certain now that she was right: it was the devil.)

Dad would hit me and say, "Get out of my sight." He'd hit me until he got tired of hitting me. I never took my eyes off of him either. Sometimes I'd cry and scream, but always my eyes were penetrating his eyes with hate. I knew he couldn't stand my eyes glaring at him, and that gave me a source of satisfaction and sick sense of power.

Grandma Lambert helped me a lot. She only lived about ten blocks away so I visited her quite often. She would buy me clothes and shoes at the Salvation Army. How I loved her for that. I was her favorite (or at least I thought so). The reason was because I spent time with her, and I was making an effort to be with her. I'd go to her house and do her dishes or housework and she appreciated it. At home there never seemed to be any appreciation. I did some of the house cleaning. The kids outside would come and holler, "Can John come out?" Mother's reply was: "If he gets the work done, he can come out."

After a while I quit trying to get done with the dishes, because if I got done with the dishes then I had to scrub the floor. If I got done with that, I had to baby-sit or change a diaper. I would have to do this or that. I never seemed to come to the end of things. I suppose much of that was because I was the oldest of six kids.

Jerry and I were constantly at odds with each other. He was my dad's favorite—the smart one. I was the dumb one. He was the one that got piano lessons for four years. I wanted guitar lessons, but that was stupid. I wanted drum lessons, but that was stupid. Anything I wanted to do was stupid. All of this intensified my hate and rebellion.

From time to time we would have house guests. Dad would have Jerry come and play the piano for them. I really starved for that attention, but it seemed, at least to me, that I never got it.

I had a set of bongo drums that I'd bought with my baby-sitting money. Dad had company over one day and I said, "Dad, I can play my bongo drums, too." He would always shut me up. But this time I was so persistent and kept interrupting: "Dad, I can play my bongo drums, too."

Finally, he said, "Go get them."

I was trying to play the drums with no accompaniment, and the people were laughing at how stupid this was. Then Dad made a complete fool out of me in front of everybody, and I thought it was on purpose. He made me feel like the lowest thing on earth—I wanted to crawl under the rug.

By now, even though I wanted love I wouldn't let anybody know I wanted it. I wanted love from my mother, but she was having so many problems with Dad and all us kids she was certainly thinking of her own survival.

Dad had gotten some fish knives from a local gas station with special stamps. They were a cheap Japanese style with wooden handles. I'd already been in a knife fight or two. So when my brother pulled one of these on me like he was going to cut me (he was playing but seemed serious), I grabbed a knife, and before he or I knew what had happened, I laid his lip wide open. I was scared. I knew he would blackmail me with my parents. I promised to give him money, candy, some of my toys, whatever I had—anything to keep him from telling Mom and Dad what had happened. They weren't going to believe me, and I knew it. He never told on me.

When we were a little older, we were skating at the lake. We had a couple of six-packs of beer and some girls. We were kissing—nothing serious. Jerry had a couple of beers too many. He started acting crazy and began to curse me. I was the tough guy in the neighborhood, and I surely wasn't going to let my little brother curse me. Twice I skated up to Jerry and grabbed him and said, "If you don't shut up, I'm going to punch you out."

"I'm sorry. I won't do it anymore, John," he replied. Then he did it again!

I skated over to him, belted him so hard he didn't know what hit him. He fell and his head hit the ice. He was knocked out for about a half hour. I was scared to death. I wasn't scared about him dying so much as I was of what was going to happen to me if he did. When he came to he ran off into the woods and fell asleep on a snowbank for about an hour. I stayed there with him and tried to wake him up but to no avail. Finally when he came to, I talked him out of telling Mom and Dad. I don't know what all it cost me, but it certainly was a lot.

I was so jealous of Jerry that I was almost possessed with envy. I was jealous of him playing the piano, looking at the little black dots with sticks on them and knowing what they said. He made pretty music come out of that thing, and I hated him for that. I desperately wanted to get Jerry in trouble. I wanted to kill myself and somehow put the guilt and blame on him.

I stood on the bridge for hours one day wanting to jump. I wanted to so badly! But I was afraid that I'd go to hell. I was so lonely and wanted so desperately to be loved. I didn't jump, only because of fear, not lack of desire. I thought I was always wrong. I thought I was so bad. *That's why nobody likes me—I'm bad, I'm no good. Everybody tells me I'm no good, so I must not be any good,* I thought. I seemed to be in a state of depression day after day. Suicide was always on my mind. I rigged up a rope on the pipes that came out by the ceiling in the bathroom. I had the rope around my neck and tried to trick my brother into kicking the stool out from under me. I thought if I could get him to do that I would have killed two birds with one stone. I would have gotten out of the picture, and I didn't do it . . . *God, I didn't kill myself—my brother did it.* Not only that, but my brother would get into trouble with Mom and Dad. That was pretty sick. Only I couldn't get him to kick the stool. However, my main motive for self-destruction was rejection.

I had started smoking when I was only eight years old. One day in the laundromat with Mother I decided to confide in her. She seemed to be treating me like an adult so I said, "Mom, I'm going to tell you something: I'm smoking."

"Oh, I know that, John. I've been finding tobacco in your shirts, and I could smell it on you," she replied.

"Mom, all of my friends smoke in front of their parents" (that was a lie), "and I think I should be able to smoke in front of you—can I?"

"No, no. We'll have to talk to your dad about it."

"Oh, Mom, please don't tell Dad," I begged.

"Okay, I won't."

You guessed it—she told him.

"John," Dad called, "smoking, huh?"

"Yes, sir," I remarked trying to act big.

"Well, as long as you're smoking you might as well smoke a man's smoke." He gave me a cigar and lit it. I smoked one cigar, then another. Dad was getting upset with me because I was puffing and inhaling those cigars like a man. Then he said, "Boy, as long as you're smoking you might as well drink too."

"Boy, this is great, Dad," I said feeling high and mighty. That was all I'd ever seen my dad do—smoke and drink. I thought this is the way to become a man.

He got the booze and started pouring us shot glasses of whiskey. He'd drink one and I would drink one. I was really feeling good. I didn't realize that he was determined to make me sick; I thought he was being my buddy. Then I started to get sick, but I had such a strong will I wouldn't let him know. When he got up to go to the bathroom I ran into my bedroom, found an old bathrobe and vomited in it, wiped off my face, and went back in the living room and sat down. When he came back from the bathroom he never knew that I had left—the cigar was still glowing in my hand.

He looked at me rather startled and said, "Okay, John, that's enough for now, but we're going to do this every night when I come home from work."

The next day at school I told everybody, "Man, my dad lets me smoke and drink. I'm going to do it with him tonight when I get home. Don't you wish you had a dad like mine?"

I got home from school and eagerly waited for

him. Finally, when he came home I said, "Dad, I'm ready."

When he found out what I was talking about he knocked me from one end of the house to the other. He was furious! I never did quit smoking or even slow down; however, I never did it around my parents again. What a letdown to realize Dad was only putting me on.

The folks always sent us to Sunday school and church; but they never went with us. To prove that we went we had to show them the church bulletin. By this time I had two more brothers, and I'd take the younger kids to Sunday school and drop them off. Dad would give us each a dime or fifteen cents to put into the church offering. I'd get all the money I could and go to my friend's house and gamble with the man who was living with his mother.

The guy had scars all over him from knife fights. He had more stories about honky-tonks and things than you ever heard. I'm sure they were all true because he was quite a rounder. He was a big guy, good looking, and just lived for the flesh. One Sunday I won almost five dollars. He got so mad he pulled a knife on me and threw me out of the house. That's how I spent our Sunday school money. If I'd get drunk or get in trouble with the police (sometimes the police would be after me), I couldn't run to my own house so I'd run to my friend's house. His mother would hide me in the basement. The police would come knocking on the door, and she'd say she didn't know me or what they were talking about.

Our move to Brooklyn Center was real great. We owned a house there. I was so glad to be out of the apartment building. I determined in this school I was going to be known as "Mr. Tough Guy." Anyone that crossed me was in for serious trouble. I beat up a couple of the tough guys, and that put me in with the corrupt and rebellious. The fighting really eased up because now I had a name. I really enjoyed the tough-guy image, and took full advantage of the situation.

Girls—I always had girls around me. Love 'em and leave them—that was my motto. I had no respect for women. I treated all of my girl friends like pigs. Sometimes I'd make them walk behind me just like a pet dog. Believe it or not, most of them seemed to enjoy that rough treatment. That seemed to really impress the gang.

Things at home went from bad to worse. I was becoming more belligerent with Dad, and couldn't cope with the situation so I decided to pack up and leave home. I went to Jerry and said, "I'm leaving home. I can't stand it one more day."

"John, I want to go with you. If you don't let me go I'm going to tell the folks."

I didn't want to take Jerry with me. However, I couldn't let him blow my cover, so I took him with me. We had decided to take off when we found that Dad was going to have a party. We thought our running away would really hurt him and mess up his party. His friends got more attention from him than we ever did, at least I thought so. I had no plans of ever coming back. I took a butcher knife out of the kitchen and stuck it in my belt. We headed for the river and walked its banks for miles. We found 35 cents on the ice and bought some jam and bread. We walked along the river to South St. Paul.

By nighttime we found a sandstone cave on the river and decided it would be a good place for us to sleep. We had found some candles and used them for light, and to start a fire inside the cave. It was only twenty feet deep, but it was warm—I suppose about 50°—while it was sub-zero outside. We laid down for a good night's rest when all of a sudden a mouse came running through the cave and raced over Jerry's face. A cat came right behind chasing the mouse. Jerry went bonkers and absolutely refused to stay in the cave, so I had to take him some place else.

We went from the cave to the downtown area and went into a laundromat. A motorcycle gang was outside. They were pretty rough characters, so we didn't stay there. While we were there we did move the machines and get the money that was under them—a grand total of $1.25.

From there we went to a used-car lot and slept in a car. We stayed there until the police came by and shone a light around the lot. They normally do that, but we didn't know it. When you're running, you think the police are always after you. We got out of the car, walked a few blocks and got into another one. It was a junk car in the yard. We stayed in it and slept on the floor, huddled up, almost freezing. Man, we were cold!

Some drunks came home in another car about 3:00 A.M. and leaned on our car and scared us half to death. When they left, we got out of the car and walked aimlessly the rest of the night. Jerry was crying by now and wanted to go home. Finally I gave in and called Dad. "Dad, I'm in Sauk Centre." Sauk Centre is about 100 miles from Minneapolis. I wanted him to think we were a lot farther away than we really were. We were still in South St. Paul.

"John," he said, "you go to the police station and have them put you on a bus. I'll pay for it. You get home now!"

"No," I said, "I'm not going to do that. I'm not coming home, but I will send Jerry."

Then he screamed, "I don't give a damn about you, but if you don't bring your little brother home you're going to really be in trouble. You bring him home, and then if you want to take off you just go ahead and ruin your life. You do whatever you want, but bring Jerry home first."

He frightened me so I took my little brother home. When we got home I was sure it would be the end for me. Dad sent us up to our bedroom. They were still having the party and I don't think anybody even knew that we had run away until I had called. There was never really much done about it that time. Normally I would have really gotten slapped around.

By now I was so rebellious that they couldn't do anything with me. I'd sneak out of the window at night, meet my buddies, steal cars, steal cigarettes, be picked up by the police and hide the cigarettes in the back seat of the squad car. They'd take us in and frisk us for whatever else we'd stolen. I was now almost crazy with rebellion.

Mom, bless her, was trying to encourage Dad and me to get along. School was a bore, and my grades were falling. Dad said he'd let me smoke at home if I'd get my grades up. I still didn't get my grades up, and I became even more rebellious. He'd come home and scream and holler at me. I know now I most likely deserved it. Sometimes I'd go to bed as early as six o'clock, trying to be in bed before he got home because I'd be afraid of what was going to happen. Maybe I had it coming, but I still lived in a hate-fear syndrome.

Mom talked Dad into buying me a Moped. Boy, I thought that was something. I suppose they thought it would help me get my grades up. With the Moped I was really a big shot around town, and I had more girl friends than ever. Sex and girls now became a way of life. No love—just physical fulfillment.

There was one girl I had sex with all the time. When I quit going with her and started going with the other girls she was jealous and told her girl friend that she was pregnant—hoping that she would tell me. Instead, her girl friend told her mother. The next thing I knew the police came to the house and picked me up. She had told her mother that I had raped her. I went to jail.

There was a real nice little kid killer in the cell next to me—about eight years old. He had killed both of his parents with a knife while they slept. This was the kind of people that were in this jail.

I had somewhat of a simulation of a trial. The judge said I'd be sent to reform school. I wasn't allowed to talk during the trial. I was sent to Woodview Detention Center and was told they were going to hold me there until I was sixteen and then send me to Stillwater, the state penitentiary.

One of the guards had closed the handcuffs too tight on my hands and they turned blue. They were afraid of gangrene or something so they took them off as soon as we reached the detention center. Right off I got smart with one of the guards. Two of them took me into the men's bathroom and beat me until I vomited. One held me while the other hit me in the guts. They really worked me over.

I was put in a cell by myself. After they shaved my head they gave me army-looking clothes and tennis shoes without laces. I couldn't believe this was happening, because I hadn't done anything. I had had sex with this girl several times, but it certainly wasn't rape by any stretch of the imagination. If it was rape, she'd raped me the first time I'd met her.

I thought, *This is America. I'm going to be set loose any day; they can't do this to me.* So when the guards were talking I was smarting back to them, telling them: "You guys are going to be sorry because I don't belong here." Well, I know now that I should have been there for a dozen other things anyway.

I had nothing. My cell was a cement slab with a mattress on it, a stool and a sink. That was it! Nothing! No sheets, no pillows, blankets—nothing. In a few days I started to submit to the system. They fed me in a room with no silverware. If they had soup, I had soup. If they had peas, I had peas, but I had to eat with my fingers, or lap it up like a dog. After they broke me—in a week or so—I got to go out into the room to eat with the rest of them. I stood at attention, walked in, sat down and ate.

I started working there by helping stack stuff in the cooler. Soon I got a few privileges. Once a week I could go out and play Ping-Pong. It was a co-ed institution. The girls were in one wing, and the boys in the other, and they'd bring us together for Ping-Pong. There was a colored guy and a white girl going at it while the guards were hitting them in the back with sticks. It was like an animal house.

During the state inspection everything was run differently—the way they treated us, the food, the whole atmosphere. Normally it was like a jungle, but during the inspection everything was smooth and a big lie.

I went to see a psychiatrist, which was the standard operating procedure, I suppose. He asked me about sex, all about this and that. I felt like the guy was really weird. He was Swedish and had the accent. To me it was like something out of a comic book. I played the guy along. I started talking to him with an accent and really getting crazy. He finally got so mad he cussed me with every name in the book, and hollered at the guard to come and get me. It took him quite a while to know that I was playing him along. Then, all of a sudden, it hit him that I was making a fool out of him and he came undone. Later on, at the second trial, his testimony was that I had the sex mind of a twenty-five year old man. I was only fifteen years old, but I thought that was pretty cool—even though I was in jail for rape.

I spent three weeks there. I certainly learned some things about discipline and about keeping my mouth shut. After three weeks the trial was up again. I don't understand what all happened. I went before the judge, and the girl told the truth. It was not during the trial, but apparently some place along the line the judge found out the truth. The judge still charged me with carnal knowledge because I was a year older than the girl, and he gave me one year probation.

Was I thankful to get out of that place. I went back to school, baldheaded and tougher than ever! My shoulders were back—ready to take on anybody because I had been to reform school. School just didn't work. I couldn't get along with anybody, so I quit—which my probation officer told me would be okay. He said, "John, you're simply wasting your time anyway. If you want to quit school, go ahead."

Dad wouldn't sign for me to quit school, but the probation officer had told me to go ahead. I don't know whether he signed or what, but he okayed it for me to get out of school. I'm sure the school officials were glad to get rid of me anyway as I was a troublemaker. Later on I went back to the school with some friends and a teacher grabbed me and really started working me over. I hit him, and put him on his knees. I was told to stay off the school grounds or I would be sent to jail.

I got a job at a manufacturing company and was taking the bus back and forth to work every day. About that same time I got hit by a dump truck and got hurt pretty bad. My motorcycle was totaled. We went to court, but I didn't get anything. Because of that wreck I ended up with back trouble, and until this day occasionally have pain.

After the wreck I'm out and Dad tells me to be in at ten o'clock. I was at a friend's house and goofing around but was home at ten. My friend walked home with me. We were in my bedroom. Dad came in, and a few minutes later called for me to come to the living room. When I got there he asked, "Where have you been?"

"I've been home since ten o'clock," I said.

"You're a blankety-blank liar," he responded. "I went over to your friend's house to pick you up." He didn't see my friend standing around the corner from where I was sitting. He started talking about how my friend's mother was some kind of a pig, how she had come to the door in a negligee, how she tried to turn him on. "Boy, I could have done this or that." The whole time my friend was standing right around the corner hearing all this. I didn't know what to do.

Dad continued arguing and hollering at me.

"Dad," I said, "I was home at ten o'clock." He drew back and started to hit me. I screamed, "Dad, don't ever try to hit me again. Never hit me again!" I pointed at him, and put my hands up to fight. He couldn't believe it because I'd never talked back to him before. I talked back to Mother one time, and she wore me out with a coat hanger. Here I was, looking him right in the eyes, saying, "Don't you ever touch me again. Never. That's it. If you lay a hand on me again I'll kill you."

He couldn't believe it and came after me. I went crazy and was screaming, "I'll kill you, you S.O.B. I'll kill you." That's all I could say.

We went crazy. We broke the sink board. We broke a couple of three chairs. He put me right through the middle of the kitchen table. Then I thought, *This is it. This is my chance. He'll have to kill me because I'm going the whole route.* I screamed again, "I'll kill you, you S.O.B. I'll kill you!" He thought that was so funny, for he had taught me to be tough.

Here I was getting my chance, and all the hate that had built up in me was now erupting! I'd practiced karate, judo, and soon had him in a strangle hold on the floor. He turned blue, and was just about unconscious. I was going to kill him. Not knowing he was drunk, I kept screaming, "I'll kill you. I'll kill you. I'll kill you."

Mom was kicking me in the back, but I didn't even know it. We were in front of the phone and she was trying to get over the two of us to get to the phone. Now everything was still, but I was still choking him and yelling, "I'll kill you. I'll kill you."

Something told me to turn him loose. When I did, it took him a couple of minutes to get up. He was all hunched over, staggered into the other room, and started crying. I had never heard my father cry before.

Mother then came to me and said, "You're a no-good son. Nobody hits his dad. You rotten kid. I've been married to your father sixteen years, and I never heard him cry. It took you to make him cry. You rotten, no-good son."

I went to my bedroom and bawled and bawled. I was so ashamed, I didn't know what to do. What's going to happen to me? I wondered.

My friend had run out of the house, and the next day told everybody in school that I killed my dad. Matter of fact, later someone asked me if I did kill him because they didn't know if I had or not. When this kid left, things were really hot and heavy.

Dad didn't talk to me about the fight, and to this day has never mentioned it. I was so ashamed of myself.

My brother was proud of me because I stood up to Dad. There was something in me that almost made me feel good; but there was more that made me feel rotten. I felt good because I whipped him; yet I felt rotten because I hit my father.

I couldn't stand the environment. It was just terrible. I was more or less told I would have to leave. I wanted that freedom anyway, so I moved in with my father's mother—still in rebellion and full of hate.

Jerry, Mother, John

3
AIRBORNE INFANTRY

Grandma was a saint, and I loved her. She knew what had happened, but never talked about me beating Dad, only that we had gotten in a fight. The fact was that I'd almost killed him. She's the kind that didn't want to say anything—forget about it; it will go away.

I knew that I was no good, but I tried never to do anything wrong when I was with Grandma. She trusted and loved me so much. I wouldn't do anything to hurt her. My grandparents weren't used to having anybody living with them, so I only stayed a couple of weeks.

Dad had a friend that worked with him who had a farm up north. Dad had told him, "Hey, my kid's all screwed up. Could you use him on your farm?"

"Well, send him to live with us—I'll take that rebellion out of him," he said. So I moved to northern Minnesota.

They were drinkers. They had a boy a couple of years older than me that was a feminine sissy.

He'd cheat and lie, was good for nothing, and he'd steal my car (by this time I had a car that I'd paid for). Or at least that's the way I felt about him. While there I got a job working for the Forestry Department. I was getting a buck and a quarter an hour—that was good money back then. It was a job mostly for derelicts that were high school dropouts. I guess in reality that's exactly what I was, or at least becoming. They'd give us an ax and take us out in the woods to clear and clean the forest.

One day their boy stole my car again, and I called him an S.O.B. The mother of the boy heard me and said, "I'm no bitch."

I said, "I didn't mean that. I'm sorry. I didn't mean that he was literally one." She was looking for a excuse to put me out and when her husband came home she told him what I had said. He called me over and said, "John, you have got to leave. No one is going to talk that way around my wife."

"I'm sorry. Man, I'm leaving," I said. "You don't understand. None of you understand. Your kid hot wires and steals my car every time he wants to." It was too late. They wanted me out! I left and went to Onamia, that was near to an Indian Reservation about fifteen miles away, where I had made some friends.

Danny, my friend said, "Hey, John, ask my brother if you can build a cabin on his property. He doesn't care."

So I talked to Jim, his brother. "Yeah, John, go ahead, do what you want."

Soon I had a little eight-by-ten-foot cabin. It had just enough room for a hide-a-bed. This was "real living." One girl after another—booze, living it up day and night. Strange...even though my dad wasn't around I was still full of hate, discontentment and rebellion. I stayed in my cabin for several months, but my money ran out, and I wanted some of the action of the city. So I went back to Minneapolis and worked at a department store. I'd still go back to the cabin on weekends.

I started working in the basement at the department store. That's where I really learned to steal. I'd always stolen, but there it was better merchandise. A guy that worked with me showed me how to do it—how to get it out without getting caught. I'd get Pendleton shirts, electric razors—you name it. I gave my dad an electric razor that I had stolen. I told him I bought it off a bum. I was still trying to be friends with him when I was around him, but that wasn't very often.

When I met these guys in the basement, I said, "I don't know where I'm going to live. I can't live with my folks any longer. My cabin is in northern Minnesota, and that's too far to drive back and forth every day. I'm looking for a one-room efficiency apartment."

"Hey, while you are looking, move in with us. We've got lots of room, and you can help pay the rent," they said.

"Wow! That sounds good."

It was a big old house over by the Minneapolis

Institute of Art. It was full of cast outs. A girl that lived on the second floor was looking for somebody to move in with her—so I did. She had had a baby that she'd given away and was about five years older than me. She bought me clothes and treated me like a king. Then she started trying to control me, telling me what time to come in, what to do, what not to do. I didn't like that. "I'm getting out of there," I said.

"Well, move in with us up here," one of the guys said. It was one floor up from the gal I left, so when I wanted sex or something, all I had to do was go downstairs.

When I moved in with these two guys I found out that one was a homosexual. And the other guy had syphilis in the third degree, and he was going crazy. Their sister lived with them, too, and was pregnant. Talk about a hell hole. I moved in dead center. Everything in that building was crazy: booze, drugs, sex. I was drunk for sure, but I never fooled with dope up to this time. I wore a bear-skin rug with a big knife stuck in my belt. That's all I wore. These hippies think they've got something new—I was crazier than they, and this was many years ago. I would run around the block dressed in this bear-skin rug. The police had seen us, and knew that there was a crazy party going someplace. They thought also that we were heavy into drugs. We weren't. The girls that came there were taking drugs. We didn't know where they had gotten them—and we didn't care. We weren't involved in it. We just were drunk!

Pretty soon the plainclothesmen came driving up and put us up against the car.

We had stolen a bunch of stuff out of the apartment house: such as busts of Michael-angelo. It was an old-time apartment house with this kind of stuff around. We decided we were going to go to California and were packing the car when the cops came up and said, "Boys, you've got to return all this stuff."

We did.

They asked what we were doing.

We said we were going to California.

"We'll be glad to get rid of you!" they said, and escorted us out of town.

What a trio: A guy with syphilis, a homo, and me—weird, sick and full of hate. Between the three of us we thought we had enough money to get us as far as Colorado. The car was a burned-out Ford with very little power. Talk about a sick and crummy lot—that we were.

I was only sixteen but had a fake identifica-tion. In Colorado if you are twenty-one you can drink booze. If you are eighteen, you can only drink beer. We were in a club in the mountains that served drinks like that. Dick (the homo), Buddy, and I were satisfied drinking our beer. Dick was about nineteen and looked a lot older. He was a wrestler, a big strong guy so they served him booze. He had not gotten the syphilis treated because he didn't know he had it until it was in the advanced stage. I don't know whether it has killed him by now or not. All I know is that when I got to know him, he told me he had syphilis in the third degree.

I had asked, "What's that mean? Go get it treated."

"You don't know much about syphilis. I go to the doctor regularly, but there is almost nothing they can do for me." He blamed girls for getting it, and as a result, he liked to give it back to any girl he could.

Dick tried to slip us whiskey, but I wouldn't drink any. The waitress saw him, came over and said, "Look, man, I told you, don't give them whiskey. It's going to get us in trouble."

Dick did it again. Finally Buddy took a shot. The waitress had been watching us. After Dick did that she sent a policeman over and all hell broke loose. Dick hit that cop before he knew what had happened. He began to put the boots to him and kicked and kicked him. I knew he was going to kill him and screamed, "Leave him alone. Let's get out of here. Leave him alone."

Buddy went behind the bar and started loading up with bottles of wine and whiskey. There I was in the middle of it, and I didn't want anything to do with any of it, but there I was anyway.

I ran out and started the car. Soon they came running and piled into the car laughing. As I was driving, I knew there was going to be a road block around every curve, and they didn't care! They were laughing and joking, passing the booze back and forth. I didn't drink any because I was trying to drive on the icy road and drive as fast as I could. I drove all night without stopping. I was scared to death. Oh God, I was scared. I mean I was scared. I knew I was in trouble. I knew I was with some guys that didn't care about anything.

Our next stop was Las Vegas. I walked into the Sands Hotel and said to the waiter, "Man, I need a job."

He said, "Well, I can probably get you one for about $1,000."

"Are you serious? I need a job now."

"Well, that's what it costs you to get a job around here—about $1,000."

I couldn't believe it. I had cleaned up and had a sports jacket on and really looked sharp. This was big time for me. To continue my act as a big shot, I decided to take the elevator to the top floor.

A lady got on the elevator also and said, "Push number 19, please," and gave me a big smile.

I said, "Yes, ma'am," and pushed the button.

"You're from the north, aren't you?" she asked.

"Yes, ma'am. I'm from Minneapolis, Minnesota."

"Well, I'm from Michigan," she said. "Come on up to my room and have a drink."

I looked at the bellboy and he shrugged. He knew I needed money so he said, "Go on up." So I did.

I thought she wanted somebody to shack up with her. She looked to be about fifty-five years old, and I really thought that was what she wanted, but she didn't. She absolutely wanted a friend. I became her friend, and she started giving me money. I'd give some of it to my friends. They were sleeping in the car while I was living it up in a penthouse. She took me to casinos and gave me all the money I could spend. She just kept laying it out saying, "Bet this on such and such. Try this on that." I mean I never had such a ball in my life. I was somewhat afraid to even go into a casino because—remember I was only sixteen! This is big time, I thought. Money—I had never seen so much money in my life. There were free drinks. All these half-naked gals were running around giving you free drinks to keep you gambling. I loved it!

She told me she was going to go back to Michigan, and she wanted me to come with her. I thought, That would be neat, but I hate to leave my friends. Can you believe that I thought these creeps were "my friends"?

Then she told me she had leukemia, and the doctors only gave her three months to live.

Then it ended. One of her sons came and tried to make out she was incompetent. They cursed me and told me to get the h— out of there—so I did—and fast! Before I left she gave me a $100 bill. She would have given me all she had, but I wouldn't take any more. I wrote her after that for a long time, and she wrote me back. Finally she quit writing. I suppose she died.

From Las Vegas we finally got to California. I had now turned seventeen, and was trying to get into the navy. My uncle was a big shot with the navy and was trying to help me enlist. They didn't want to take me because of my record. He was trying to get my record waived and wasn't having any luck with that.

Buddy wanted to find his mother, and when he did he discovered she was a prostitute run by two old men. They were winos. She was about forty and looked sixty. They were sixty and looked eighty. They had beaten her up the day we got there, so we went in and beat them up. I took a cane away from one of them and broke a gallon of whiskey that was on his table, broke his television set and destroyed practically everything in the apartment.

Buddy was so upset that his mother was a whore that he went out and was trying to kill himself.

Dick yelled, "I've got to go. Stop him! He's going to kill himself!" They ran out, and about that time the police came in the back door. I ran into the bathroom and jumped in the tub. The bathroom window was already opened because one guy had just gone out the window. I jumped in the tub and pulled back up behind the shower curtain. A cop kicked the door open and brought that gun around in my face. He looked but never saw me. He turned around and walked out.

I was trembling. Man, I didn't want to go to jail. They stayed there—it seemed like hours—but I know it couldn't have been over ten minutes and then left.

Buddy's mom came back to the apartment,

and these bums started to beat her up again. I came out of the bathroom like a rocket. I told them that I'd kill them if they ever touched her again. They were petrified because we had already destroyed the house and beat them up once—this would have been the second time around.

I went to school there for a while and worked at odd jobs. During this time I was still trying to get into the navy. I couldn't afford to live on my own. I wasn't a homosexual, and I didn't want anything to do with Buddy any longer.

Dick was getting crazier. He was getting into fights almost every night. We'd go to McDonalds, and he'd start trouble with somebody over the slightest thing. Finally I knew I had to get away from them because I was going crazy just being around them. I was drunk on wine every night, or almost every night. I was getting into deep trouble, and I knew it! I would soon be a seventeen-year-old wino.

I humbly called home and said, "Dad, I want to come home. I want to join the army; the navy won't take me."

Dad sent me a bus ticket via Western Union. He was showing me love, but again I just couldn't see it.

I took the bus home. I was sent down to the army recruiter, but they said, "No way, man, no way." It really took the wind out of my sails and right fast.

Dad didn't want to see me end up in prison, and thought if I got in the army it would be better. That's what I was thinking too. I really wanted to make something of myself. I had screwed up everything so far, and I wanted to straighten up, so we went to St. Paul to the judge. The army needed soldiers then because they were really getting slaughtered good in '66. I got a waiver from the judge, and he cleared my record and said, "If you go in the army from here, everything will be all right."

At the recruiting office, the guy ahead of me went "airborne." I asked the sergeant, "What's 'airborne'?"

"You get paid $55 more a month, and you jump out of airplanes," he answered.

I was so dumb that I thought you had to be smart to jump out of airplanes. I thought that would be for someone with an education. I signed up for it—airborne—but said, "I want electronic maintenance engineering. I'm volunteering so that I can get that, right?"

"Right," the sergeant said with a smile. He was lying to me, because as soon as you sign up for "airborne" it waives anything else. They put me in the airborne infantry. As soon as we signed up the recruiters started laughing and joking.

"What's so funny?" I asked.

"I want to tell you something, boys," he replied. "There's only two things that come out of the sky—idiots and bird crap. Which are you?"

I knew then that I'd done something wrong!

I was sworn in, and I knew that my life was a

whole new ball game. *I've never succeeded in anything in my life, so I'll be the very best I can,* I thought.

Within a short time, I found that being airborne waived my electronic maintenance training that I wanted. That kind of broke my heart because I wanted to become something; to get an education where I could amount to something.

After I signed up I still had a week before I was to report to Fort Leonard Wood. The day before I was to report for duty, I went wild. I was like a wild animal who knows he is going to be caged. Everything seemed to go wrong in my '50 Pontiac. I was getting the oil changed, and while my friend was lowering the car on the hoist he left a fifty-five gallon drum there and the door was open. The door caught on the fifty-five gallon drum left in the way, and it peeled up the bottom of the door as the car came down. I was sick about it, but I went out on a date anyway.

After I dropped my date off, I picked up two girls on the street who were into drugs and sex. I had a case of beer in the car so we went down by the river and parked. I thought I was in heaven. I'd never been with two girls before.

Later on that night, dead drunk, I was seeing how many stop signs I could run. I ran one going about seventy, and almost hit a patrol car. When the officer measured my skid marks he said, "They are about sixty feet. Boy, if I have my way you will go to jail and never get out."

The girls were not helping the situation. They offered the policemen beer and invited them to come in the car and have a party.

"We're going to take you in. If you've got an ace in the hole, you'd better play it now, kid," they taunted.

"I've got one," I said and reached up above the visor. I pulled out the papers stating I was going into the service the very next day.

"Man, that's the only ace you could have to keep you out of jail." At that time they told me to get out of there and not cause any more trouble.

The next day boarding the train for Fort Leonard Wood I was scared to death.

The first day they shaved our heads and told us that we were nothing, lower than nothing— we weren't even dogs. I thought basic training was really rough, but the more I was there the easier it got. As your body gets in better physical shape, it is not nearly as strenuous on you.

I did do a lot of dumb things, like showing up in formation one day with gum in my mouth, and, of course, I got caught. After training that day the sergeant came to me and said, "Steer, dig a hole six feet deep and bury your gum." This was after hours when I should have been polishing my shoes, showering, and getting ready for the next day.

I buried the gum, and the next day during formation the sergeant asked, "Did you bury that gum, private?"

"Yes, sir, I did."

He said, "You look like a liar to me. I don't believe you. Tonight when we get done training, I want you to dig it up and show it to me."

I thought I would die, but needless to say, I never chewed gum in formation again.

About a month later I got pneumonia and went out of my head with fever. It was very cold during the winter at Fort Leonard Wood. I wasn't going to report for sick call because a guy who reported for sick call was considered a sissy and was harrassed. They had to carry me out of my bed delirious to the hospital. I was only there a couple of days, and then it was back to the same routine.

I was in formation, exhausted, and didn't think that I could make it. I was standing at attention and fell asleep while standing there and dropped my rifle. The sergeant caught it right away. He made me do one hundred push-ups, and each time I did one I had to kiss my rifle and say, "I love my rifle. I will not drop my rifle. I love my rifle. I will not drop my rifle. I will not drop my rifle." I thought it was ridiculous but I learned a lot. It wasn't long before I started getting a little pride in my outfit. It seemed our outfit always had the best this, the best that, so we had to work that much harder to get the banners and the trophies.

Before I got through basic they were already talking about the paratroopers. They no longer made fun of me because they were trying to get

the rest of the guys to sign up. Being a paratrooper was really the elite thing to do. It was
for the tough guys.

After boot camp I was assigned to the
airborne infantry. This was a special infantry for
paratroopers. Regular infantry might qualify
with a few rifles and a little of this and that, but
we were more specialized and qualified in twenty
different ways. We learned how to kill people in
over 100 different ways. The standard operating
procedure was to learn to use a knife, piano wire,
etc., to kill! The violence and hate seemed to
increase with such intensity that at times I was
frightened by it. This was evidenced when I
went home for a short leave after basic training.

I picked up some other soldiers and we had a
case of Canadian whiskey in the car. We picked
up three girls at a drive-in. They said, "We're
having a party at our house, let's go there."
Naturally we said, "That sounds great, sure,
let's go."

What the girls were wanting was our case of
whiskey—not us. As it turned out, it wasn't
their house but a house rented by a bunch of
college guys. There were about fifteen guys
there and a couple of girls getting drunk.

As soon as we went in, we realized that we'd
been had. One of the guys got rowdy and threw
a whiskey bottle through the apartment
window. The college guys got rough with us and
cussed us out.

I went bananas and screamed, "Come on outside and fight."

They had us outnumbered, but we didn't care. We were soldiers and all psyched up. I pulled a knife on a guy, and as I did, he stuck a .38 in my stomach. "Hey, man," I said, "take it easy." These guys were really mad now. I put the knife in my pocket very slowly. "You don't want to kill somebody. Hey, I'm sorry. I'm sorry. You guys, tell them you are sorry. We just want to go. We don't want any trouble."

Just then another guy walked out of the house with a shotgun and leveled it right on my head. I was almost sweating blood. I had a .38 in my guts, and another was holding a 12-gauge on my head.

"Let's go, guys, they can have the whiskey. It's not worth getting wasted over."

We left, and I trembled all the way home. *Will I ever learn?* I thought.

Airborne infantry was as close to hell as I ever want to experience. The training was intense and laced with deep webs of competition— turning everybody against everybody. We soon became and were treated like animals. It was all so bizarre, crazy, but yet real. I'd run around the streets screaming, "Kill, kill, kill. Kill VC. I want to be an airborne ranger, living on blood and guts and danger."

We got perhaps four hours sleep, and the rest of the day was brainwashing, calisthenics, hand-to-hand, and all the different types of training in plastic explosives. Blindfolded we would break down a dozen different kinds of weapons and learn the parts and how to put them together. We'd had a taste of that in the regular training in basic, but it wasn't the intensity and spirit. Basic was just everyone trying to get through it and get their AIT, which might be type clerk, signal corp., or some kind of education.

The men that trained us lived for it. They'd call us the filthiest names, kick us right square in the rump for no reason at all. They'd hurt you and drop you for pushups until you thought your arms were going to give way. Then they'd put their foot on your back and push you and make you give some more.

We hardly ever walked on the floor in the barracks. We would hop from bed to bed. Every day we polished the floor and then buffed it with a sheepskin.

In formation one day, they took my belt buckle and looked on the inside of it. I had used "brasso" on the inside with a Q-tip. The sergeant found a cotton fiber from the Q-tip. I stood there breathless with my heart pounding, knowing I was in trouble. One little quarter-inch long fiber from a Q-tip hair inside my belt buckle, and man, you'd thought I had shot the President. When he got done cursing and dressing me down, he made me run a mile and a half back to the company screaming at the top of my lungs, "I am a jackass. I am a jackass. I am a jackass."

Their entire strategy was to run us out now if we couldn't take it. When the real thing hit in

Vietnam, they wanted people that could stick it out no matter what happened, and people that would take orders blindly without thinking or considering the outcome. They wanted you to react to whatever was said—and now!

One of the guys in the outfit, by the name of Sid, was a golden glove champion. One of the sergeants found out about this. He said to the kid, "You don't like me, do you?"

Sid replied, "It's not my job to like you, sergeant. You're my teacher, and I will do what you tell me."

The sergeant pushed Sid and said, "But really, you don't like me do you? You hate my guts, don't you?"

Finally Sid said, "Yes, sergeant, I hate your guts."

"You'd like to kick the dickens out of me, wouldn't you?"

"No, sergeant. I don't want any trouble. I just want to get through this training. I don't want any trouble."

The sergeant kept pushing him saying, "Really, you'd just like to kick the dickens out of me, wouldn't you?"

"Well, I would. I'd like a crack at it sometime, but I'm not going to get in trouble over it."

The sergeant said, "You follow me." He took him off into the woods. The sergeant was an expert in karate and brought Sid back over his shoulder and dropped him in front of us.

The diabolical and degrading training was this hand-to-hand combat with padded-on-ends sticks. They would form us in a circle and call us out to fight. If the sergeant didn't like you (they were always picking somebody out to make an example of—if you had red hair, if you had an airborne ring, if you had a tattoo—just anything to make an example of you) he would call you out over and over. There would always be two guys in the middle fighting. Two minutes of this was enough to wear anybody out. You'd be getting hurt and using everything you had in your body. The sergeants were proficient at it, and they'd really hurt you. They'd hit you in the groin a couple of times—in the head—knock you down with the wind knocked out of you—and they'd stand above you laughing, or kicking sawdust in your face until you'd get up.

As soon as you would attempt to get up they would knock you back down. If there was somebody they didn't like, they'd get him in the circle and work him over. So they wouldn't get in trouble being the ones that beat him up they'd team you off with your buddy, then they would all holler: "Kill him. Kill him." The competition would take over and you would want to kill your own buddy. If the sarge really wanted to get you, he would. They'd give the stick to another guy, another guy, and another guy. One guy might have to fight four, five or six guys. He'd get so tired that he could hardly move and be battered beyond belief. I went through this and it was terrible.

Our training became progressively more strenuous. There were times I thought I would lose my sanity. My hatred and bitterness became more complex the longer I trained. One incident stands out most vividly in my mind. The drill was to take a man's weapon away and disarm him. In this instance—his rifle.

We were taken to a sawdust pit about 200 feet long, paired off and placed about twenty feet apart. There was a sergeant watching every two pairs. We no more had hit the sawdust until my partner came at me like a madman screaming at the top of his voice, "Ke-yaa!."

Instantly I wanted to kill him and gave him a karate chop to his head. I grabbed his hands, and then I flipped him to the ground. I heard him scream again, but this time it was pain causing the wail. There was blood all over his face. My heart raced with excitement, and yet fear gripped me that I had really killed him.

Just then I was hit on the back and I jerked to attention as the sergeant yelled, "That's the way to do it, kill 'em. That's how you do it, boy!"

He then looked down at the guy in the sawdust. He bent over, cursed him, jerked him up and said, "Get your ass over to the infirmary. Get your head sewed up and get back here fast. Do you understand me, soldier?"

"Clear, Sergeant. Airborne!" was the faint reply.

My emotions were fast becoming seared. The sergeant saying, "That's the way," overshadowed any feeling of remorse or pity. Pride and arrogance swelled within me as I pondered: *Yes, airborne isn't for the weak. It's for a real macho man like me.*

The apex of the airborne infantry training was we had to go through an escape and evasion course which was a simulated Vietnamese war zone. There were Vietnam villages, artillery fire, wire, booby traps, etc. The sergeants and other officers were the "Vietnamese." This course was run after dark. We were given a map individually, not as an outfit. This was one against the Cong. Every man was out for himself. We weren't fighting together.

We'd heard a lot about what went on in the dark. Guys were getting their arms broken and even being tortured. If you were captured, you were taken to a Vietnamese village. They'd chain logs around your legs and make you march with these logs attached. The object was not to get caught. You weren't supposed to really hurt anybody, but everybody did.

We were given blank bullets. I was scared, and yet so determined that I was going to get through it without getting caught. The first ones through got a pat on the back. There were 300 of us that were determined that we were all going to be number one.

The course was a death-defying ten miles long. I set my face like flint and faded into the midnight darkness. Within minutes I could hear men yelling as they were taken prisoners and herded into the waiting trucks. They would first be taken to a camp where they tried to get them to give more than their name, rank and serial number. They really worked them over trying to break them. I never saw so many guys with black eyes and bruises as after this course was over.

I estimated I was about halfway through when suddenly from out of nowhere a lieutenant jumped up, put his rifle on my head and said, "I've got you, soldier. You're caught."

Terror overcame me as I kicked him in the groin and hit him on the side of his face with the butt of my gun. It was dark so I knew he couldn't identify me. I took off running like a deer. *No one will ever take me and live*, I thought. I crawled between them. To me it was no longer a game. It was real war! Finally I saw the lights of the lodge. I had made it! I had made it! My reward was a cup of hot chocolate and the pat on the back. I was number thirty-one in, so that put me in with the goody-goodies.

The next day at formations it looked like most of the men had just returned from the front lines. The men had broken hands, fingers, black eyes, and what have you. The lieutenant stood at attention like a statue. He never said one word about his black eye—but I sure knew how he got it!

By the time I graduated from AIT, I thought I was "IT." I was the toughest in the world—except I didn't have my wings yet. I still wasn't a paratrooper—jump school was next.

4
JUMP SCHOOL

There were tests and more tests. Many were screened out—they just couldn't stand the strain. Those of us that made it felt tougher and more elite. I had Osgood-Schlatters disease in my knees and wasn't supposed to be running. I was operating on pure grit, pure hate and competition. If it killed me, I was going to get through jump school.

Jump school was held at Fort Benning, Georgia. Again it was the same thing. I had thought that AIT (Advanced Individual Training) was rough until I got to jump school. AIT was a breeze to what I was now enduring.

One neat thing about jump school was that all the trainees were treated alike—a general or private—it didn't make any difference, all were the same. Even if you were a general going through jump school, you were considered a dog, just an absolute dog. There aren't very many generals, of course, that go through, but there were majors training with me.

When we were put in the barracks, it was again the same thing. You don't touch the floor, etc. Here we were once again running around the streets screaming, "I want to be an airborne ranger, living on blood and guts and danger." All the way, every day, screaming and running five miles before breakfast every morning.

I got where I could really handle the run; at first I blacked out. It wasn't just running an intensive run, it was a pushed run. When I would black out, I'd wake up with somebody kicking on me: "Get up you so and so. If you can't take it, get out!"

During training there were a few preachers going through paratroopers, and they could tell the dirty jokes just like the "rest of us boys." One day we were running around the track. We had a priest who was trying to be a paratrooper. (Unfortunately, when I was in the military, I don't believe I ever met a Christian. I probably did, but they never told me they loved Jesus and were a Christian.) This priest was a little old to be going through paratrooper school. He was probably about twenty-eight, and that's an old man for the training we were going through! He couldn't make the run. By then, I was getting in pretty good shape, so I dropped back a little bit and grabbed him by the hand and said, "Come on, Father, we can make it." We were half running, and I was half dragging him.

A sergeant stopped me and called me over on the side: "Are you religious?"

"No, sergeant, I'm not religious."

"What are you doing helping that blankety-blank priest?"

"Well, I hadn't stopped running. I was still doing my running. I had just reached back and helped him a little bit."

He cursed me and said, "I'm going to get you out of the airborne. We don't need people in the airborne like you. I'm going to see that you don't make it through."

I couldn't believe what I was hearing! My intuition told me I was in for some trouble!

The very next day we were to begin our training on the swing-line trainer. This is a big steel ring that you are harnessed into. Then you are dropped any which way, continually, from about four or five feet. There are pullies hooked every way conceivable. It's a simulated landing in a parachute where you could actually land on your head if the wind was a little wrong at the last minute. They tip you every way, and you are supposed to do a PLF (parachute landing fall).

Suddenly it was my turn in the swing-line ring. My sergeant bellered, "Hey, Captain, come here. See this kid here? He's religious. He's helping the priest. Let's show him what we do to religious people."

They were always looking for somebody out of which to make an example. I never wanted to be that person. All of a sudden, there I was "that very person."

Man, they dropped me on my head. They dropped me where I'd hit that steel rim with my chin. At first they usually drop you a couple of times and let you go. To me, however, they just kept doing it, and doing it, and taunting and teasing: "What's the matter, don't you know how to land? You'll never be a paratrooper. You'll never be a paratrooper." They worked me over but good. But I had it in my heart that I was just going to be cool. I went through it. I endured it, and kept my mouth shut. Finally they let me down.

I never thought I would hear the words, "Tomorrow you jump." My heart pounded with sheer excitement and anticipation of the thought of my first jump. What would it be like to feel the wind rush by my cheeks and to see the ground looming at a death pace below me? Tomorrow I would know.

Breakfast was endless as the time of the jump approached. "All right, men," the sergeant bellered, "climb on the platform and jump."

"What's this all about?" I asked the guy standing next to me. We were then told to climb out onto a three-foot platform and jump. For a week we jumped off of the three-foot platform— hundreds and hundreds of times. If you dared to say one word you jumped a hundred more times. Everything must be done in mute obedience—so I jumped and jumped and jumped—no rushing wind, no free fall—no nothing, just three feet! They were teaching us how to land . . . but from the frightening height of three feet.

The next phase was more intriguing. The jump would now be off a thirty-four-foot trainer.

"KLUGLE, FOR THE LAST TIME-
TONIGHT. . . *IT'S ONLY THREE
FEET DOWN!*"

I put my harness on wrong the first time and it
shifted wrong in my crotch. I knew then this
was a serious life-and-death situation.

I would climb the tower, harness up, and
jump. The free fall was about twelve feet before
the cable that was attached to your harness
grabbed and jerked you as though your chute
had just opened. You then rode the cable at
thirty miles an hour to the ground.

The sergeants were there constantly with
their bullhorns cursing you. "Get back up there.
Do it again. Do it again. Watch your landing.
You will break your back, you idiot."

You continually go through this process until
you can jump off the platform blindfolded and
do what you're supposed to do without thinking.
It's like karate or anything else; after you train
over and over and over, you do a certain thing
automatically—almost without consciously
thinking about what you are doing. It becomes
instinct.

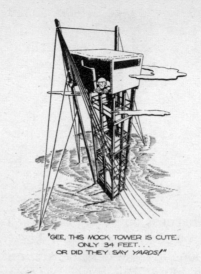

"GEE, THIS MOCK TOWER IS CUTE.
ONLY 34 FEET...
OR DID THEY SAY *YARDS!*"

The next tower would be the 250-foot one where you would be in a parachute and hoisted to the top and dropped. By this time I was a little more cautious because I knew the danger that was involved. There was not quite as much harrassment from the sergeants because some of the men were really getting hurt on this fall. If a wind came up and blew you back into the tower, and you didn't slip right or steer that parachute right, you would get wrapped around that steel tower and hurt yourself or perhaps be killed. It was fun because this was really parachute jumping. We again jumped over, and over, and over.

By this time you were so brainwashed, you truly thought, *Man, we're the best. We are the best, and everybody else is dogs.* If you'd see a "leg," which is what you called somebody that wasn't a paratrooper, you looked down on him—he was the scum of the earth.

Then came jump week. You had to make five jumps in one week. This is what we were all waiting for. You're psyched up for it. You just can't wait to do it. You are scared, but this is why you've been training for four or five months.

Before we boarded the airplane, our sarge gathered about sixty of us together and said, "Look, men, this is the day you have been waiting for. If you want to chicken out this is the time to do it, and I won't say a word. But if you get on the plane the only way you will get down is jumping out of the door in flight. Yes, by parachute. There isn't one of you that has to get on the plane."

I sat there wondering how many quitters there were going to be. There were none. We were always looking for quitters and trying to force them out because in a combat situation, you certainly don't want this kind of guy next to you. Of course, that's a good way of exalting yourself. You find somebody that's weaker than you—it makes you feel macho.

Suddenly we were on the plane and preparing to make our first jump. We were all hooked up, absolutely scared witless. We had heard all the stories about the guy that landed in the tree, the one that got killed—and soon we would be standing at the open door.

You see the blinking red light. The doors are opened on each side of the plane. We were lined up, a thirty-man line on each side. There was a jump master at each door that made sure whoever got to that doorway went out! The green light comes on and you stand in the door. You slap your hands on the door, and you're ready to go. The first jump is five-second intervals. You go and in five seconds the next guy goes . . . the next guy goes, etc.

Suddenly I realized the doors had been opened. We were really going to jump. I was tenth in line. We were told that our first jump would be in five-second intervals, and to be prepared for the prop wash that would pick us up and throw us up and behind the plane. The line started moving. We were on our way. All of the training on how to jump out of the plane was rather meaningless because the second you got to the door, the sergeant gave you a shove and you were on your way!

With a swish I was thrown up and back. The static line followed as I did a circle and started falling. The static line then ripped the chute open, and I felt the terrible jerk. I looked up and shook and checked my lines. It was beautiful. All my training, and suddenly I was in heaven flying by myself. I was 1,250 feet up in the air, and I seemed to lose my natural consciousness. Here was God's country. Paratroopers all around you, your buddies that you are going to fight with and die with. They're all floating around.

Then you start to remember things you were taught. *Oh, I can steer this thing,* and I reached up and pulled my lines down into me. It spilled the air out of the back of the chute, and I went shooooo ... floating to the left. It was breathtaking and WOW! out of sight. I grabbed another way and went back that way. It was just so neat. I thought, it's taking forever to get to the ground. Then all of a sudden, I was a hundred feet off the ground, and the ground was jumping up at me. I screamed, "What do I do? What do I do? Man, I forgot everything!" I hit the ground, and did what I was supposed to do. I had made it—my first jump! I landed harder than I expected to. I really didn't expect that my knees were going to hit my chin when I hit the ground. This was really serious but who cared? I made it.

Then I ran up and grabbed the apex of my

chute and brought it around into the wind so that it didn't drag me. I was not a paratrooper yet because I hadn't made five jumps, but man, I could do it! I could really do it. I was safe on the ground and I'd made it.

In an hour or so as we were picked up, I was well aware that quite a few had been hurt. "Hey, John," my buddy yelled, "did you hear that Jason Hill broke his ankle?"

"That's nothing, you should have seen them carry Rick away. His back was broken," another remarked.

Because of those comments and others, I started to get a little more apprehensive and leery about jumping. Now in reality, not theory, I knew one could actually be severely hurt or even killed jumping. Regardless of these facts, I was going to become a paratrooper and finish my five jumps.

The second jump was rather uneventful even though I was scared witless. The first jump was the easiest because I really didn't know what to expect. As the time approached for my third jump, the apprehension in me mounted. For some unknown reason my fear grew more anguished. When I approached the door of the airplane, I knew I had to jump even though everything in me said "Don't." Suddenly I felt the jerks of the lines, but it was different. My parachute did a cigarette roll and did not fully open. I was slowed somewhat but still plunging to my doom. I suddenly knew why I had been so apprehensive.

I had a reserve chute I could open, but if I did it could wrap around my main one. It's pretty tricky opening up a reserve, especially falling at 100 MPH. The reserve is right in front of you, and the lines and everything open right up in your face. It's not designed like the one in the back, and it's not as large. I didn't want to pull my reserve.

Next thing I knew I was sitting on top of the canopy of another man's chute. I grabbed his apex and realized that most likely both of us would be dead in a matter of minutes. I was almost in a state of panic, and this guy was cursing me and calling me every name in the book. I had his parachute about half dipped in the middle so I really couldn't blame him.

"Man, I ain't about to get off of here. There ain't no way," I screamed.

I was frantically shaking my shroud lines trying to get the chute to open, and finally it popped open. When it did, it lifted me off the parachute over to the side. Then I drifted into the top of his parachute, and it collapsed around my waist.

He was really cursing me now because I was all tied up in his shroud lines. His only salvation now was me because he was now going down by my parachute.

"Man, shut up," I yelled. "I'm doing all I can. Just shut up. Don't you know I'm trying, man. You think I like this?"

I got untangled from him about fifty foot or so above the ground when his chute fully opened.

Prior to that it was about half opened. When he got loose he drifted right under me—which took the air out of my parachute. When that happened it fell like a shot.

I didn't get hurt very bad when I fell, but it was a miracle that I didn't break every bone in my body. My knees hit my chin, and I knew I had broken my jaw. *Man, you can get killed doing this stuff,* I pondered.

I had two more jumps left. By this time every jump was getting worse. Then I was thinking: to remain on jump status I have to make at least a jump a month all the time that I'm a paratrooper. I don't know whether this is really worth it or not. But everything was so intense, and I was so brainwashed about going through it I didn't really consider seriously not doing it.

The guys that pack chutes have their names and everything on that chute. When you become a paratrooper you have the right at any time to say, "I'm not jumping with this chute. The guy that packs it jumps it." Then if there's something wrong with it, it's their life. They'd always say that if your chute didn't open, you could come back and get another one!

The last jump that I made was an equipment jump. It drove me into the ground. It really hammered me hard. I landed on the side of my head. You're not supposed to land like that, but something happened with the wind just before I hit the ground. Maybe I made a mistake, I don't know. The side of my head hit first. Then the rest of me plowed in. I had all this equipment strapped to me, and man, I got bruised up. With that jump I was a paratrooper, and one with no broken bones. What a feeling!—to stand there and let the General pin your wings on you. That was really something.

I could now go on into special forces or into the ranger school. Again, this was more of the same kind of stuff. I was hot to go to Vietnam. I wanted to go. I was going to end the war. I was going to go there and win the war. I didn't care what else was going on, I could and would do it.

Uncle Jim, John, Jerry (killed in car accident), sister Susan

5
VIETNAM

Before I shipped overseas I had a few days leave at home. All the folks came over to say good-bye. As usual, I drank too much, and my mouth got me in trouble with Dad. I really caused him a lot of grief. I was bitter and rebellious to the last minute. Dad wasn't very impressed with my going, and I couldn't blame him.

My mom's attitude was very typical: "Johnny's going off to war." Mom and Dad had high hopes of me finding myself and being a hero. I was anxious to go, but yet a little afraid.

I lost my sweetheart over going to Nam. I had quite a war with her. She gave me back the diamond ring that I had bought her. In anger I threw it out the window of the car and never did find it.

I didn't have a real sad, tearful parting. I drank and acted crazy most of my furlough.

I went from Fort Bragg to San Francisco in transit to Vietnam. I had to have a few more shots because of going into jungle conditions. I was there a few days getting paperwork cleared—and drinking in the EM Club waiting on our plane. Suddenly everything was so different because I was completely by myself. The others were all strangers. My old group got orders to different places. I was shipped out on a commercial airline. It was a long flight to the other side of the world, and to a hell hole that would almost destroy my life.

"The plane will land outside of Saigon. Be ready for anything," were the words that came over the intercom. As I looked out the window I saw small puffs of smoke. "What do you think that is?" I asked.

"We're being mortared," someone yelled. In an instant it was war, the real thing! They rushed us off the plane. The mortaring was really no big deal, but you could hear it and see the shells hitting. The pilot was wanting to get us off and get his plane out of there fast. Soon he screamed down the runway. Suddenly he was gone, and we were left to God only knew what.

I was startled by the beller of the Sergeant as he screamed, "On to the bus—hurry, hurry, hurry. Come on, soldier, move!" The bus was OD (olive drab) with screens over the windows.

"Why all the screens over the windows, Sergeant?" I asked.

"So our friends can't throw grenades in here," was his reply.

From there we went to company some place and ended up burning human refuse for about a week. They put it out in a field. You dry it, turn it over, and then burn it. It was a very exciting job! Soon I was told that I was going with the 101st Airborne Division. However, the 173d Airborne had just made a jump on Junction City 1, and they lost a few guys. They needed some replacements, so my orders were changed to the 173d Airborne Division. There again, it was all kind of spooky because I didn't know anybody there.

They had an enlisted men's club. I burned crap all day, drank beer at night. *Some war,* I thought. They had regular inspections like in the States—only in Nam things were filthier. There was no way you could have the cleanliness like Stateside.

After a week I was assigned to jungle school. It was simply another jungle in Vietnam. By this time, I had been issued a rifle. In training, we killed three Vietnamese. This was kind of fun. I didn't personally kill them. All I could see in my mind was 100 of us and one of them. *This ain't too bad odds,* I thought.

I got my patches. Was I ever proud when I received my 173d Airborne patch. The 173d Airborne Brigade (Separate) was organized 25 June 1963, from the 2d Airborne Battle Group, 503d Infantry. The brigade thus inherited the proud tradition of the 503d Parachute Infantry that jumped into combat on Corregidor in 1944.

Under the command of Brigadier General Ellis W. Williamson, the 173d trained hard on its home island, Okinawa, and throughout the Asian Theatre. Extensive airborne, guerrilla, and jungle warfare training in Taiwan, Korea, and Thailand brought the unit to a high pitch of readiness. It was from the many parachute exercises on Taiwan that the 173d paratroopers became known as the "Sky Soldiers."

As the first separate brigade in the United States Army, the 173d had to prove the validity of a new concept. Less than two years after its organization, the brigade was called upon to prove its mettle in combat. In May 1965, lead elements of the brigade with supporting equipment, ammunition, and supplies, departed Okinawa by aircraft. The remainder of the brigade deployed by ship two days later.

Since that time, the Sky Soldiers established an unparalleled record of first in the Vietnam War. The 173d was the first army ground combat unit to arrive in Vietnam, the first to enter the Iron Triangle, the War Zones "C" and "D." The Sky Soldiers spearheaded the combat effort in the Delta and the highlands, and conducted the first joint American-Vietnamese operation.

It came as no surprise then, that the 173d was chosen to make the first combat parachute assault since the Korean conflict. Even today it has earned the proud heritage it bears—it has the right to remain a separate brigade.

I was assigned to A Company, 2nd Battalion, 173d Airborne Infantry. The infantry battalion is the primary fighting force of any combat unit. It is the infantry battalion that searches out and destroys the enemy. All other units support the infantry, for, as the infantry goes, so goes the battle.

The 173d had three infantry battalions: the 1st, 2nd, and 4th Battalions of the 503d Infantry (1, 2, and 4/503d). Each 750-man battalion, with supporting artillery and armor, can operate for an extended period of time as a self-sustaining unit.

The 2nd Battalion was chosen to conduct the first parachute assault of the Vietnam War. On 22 February, 1967, paratroopers of the "We Try Harder" battalion jumped into combat to initiate Operation JUNCTION CITY.

The 4th Battalion arrived in Vietnam, 25 June 1966, and immediately joined the 173d Airborne Brigade. Under the command of Lieutenant Colonel Michael D. "Iron Mike" Healy, the men of the 4th Battalion came to join the fight. Since that time the "Geronimo" paratroopers have carved out a distinguished combat record.

The airborne infantryman wears two symbols of his accomplishments: the parachutist's wings and the Combat Infantryman's Badge. He is an elite and proud soldier—and let me tell you—I was one proud man!

I eventually made friends with them and worked my way into my part of the unit, and, finally, I started feeling like one of the boys. We made a lot of little local search and destroy missions. We learned about all the booby traps and the different ways that the enemy fought.

Our first search and destroy missions were close around the area. We'd kill a few of them.

They'd kill a few of us. It was kind of neat because we had them outnumbered so badly. We had modern equipment. We'd just be gone a few days and then it was back to the prostitutes, booze and drugs.

As time went on we were assigned larger and larger operations, and they were farther and farther away from home base. One day one of the whores in Bien Hoa told us, "I'll see you when you can get back."

"What do you mean, you'll see us when we get back? We aren't going any place," I said.

"Soldier, you're leaving tomorrow for a secret mission, and you're going to jump by parachute." We didn't know anything about that, but the next morning about 0400, we were awakened, quickly taken to the airport, gotten on the airplane and issued a parachute. It was apparent that the whores knew more about the war than we did.

We were supposed to jump, and they sent in the LRRP (long range recon patrol) ahead of us, and the gooks (North Vietnamese) killed every one of them to the man before they hit the ground. There was an ambush set up right on the jump sight. They knew exactly where we were going to jump. As a result, we didn't jump.

They jockeyed us around different places. One time we were to save the rear end of the special forces on the Black Virgin Mountains. That was kind of hairy as we went in there in helicopters. Suddenly every day now we were headed for a different encounter.

We went to the Black Virgin Mountains. That's where I got George, my monkey. When we got there everything seemed to be a mess. We got there just in time to save the Special Forces from being slaughtered. They had dropped us out on a hot LZ. As we ran out of the back of the helicopters, the gooks opened up on us. It was getting less and less like a game, and there were more and more people getting killed.

We encountered contact as we were moving back up the hill. Suddenly I heard the rat-a-tat of machine-gun fire. The guy next to me opened up with an automatic weapon. Boy, I hit the dirt! Still not a great warrior, but I hit the dirt in a prone position with my rifle.

A sergeant came up behind me, kicked me in the butt and said, "Don't you know the difference between AK-47 and an M-60?" It was one of my own men that had opened up behind me on some guy up ahead.

We screamed, carried on and ran up towards the battle. You couldn't see the enemy—you just shot. The foliage was thick in the jungle, and so was the enemy. The closer you pushed in on them, the more there were. We fought our way up the hill. We had to get to a certain point and were told we had to move that night. We didn't like moving at night. They had leaves that glowed in the dark. The only way you knew where you were going was to take one of these leaves and stick it in the guy's helmet that was ahead of you, and follow that glowing thing through the dark.

The guy pulling point would shoot in the az-miuth of the compass and just walk. He'd walk into trees, the bushes, vines, and work his way around trying to go in that general direction.

The guy behind the point would follow that little glowing thing in the dark, that's all. This was scary and dangerous. It was in the mountains, jungle-like mountains, but there were cliffs that you could slide down and have to climb up—constantly aware that you could walk right into an ambush. The gooks were in the trees. Every now and then they would open up on us. We would shoot back and hope we weren't shooting each other. I imagined all of our guys getting shot by us. It was almost beyond belief.

At one spot I grabbed two guys and said, "Dig here." We didn't have any shovels, but we had our helmets, and the three of us dug a hole.

I mean the enemy was all around us in the trees. The only thing that had saved us was the dark. Everytime they'd open up, and we'd open up, things would light up. Then they'd know where to shoot at again, and they'd shoot in that area. It was terrible. We were all scared spitless. It was just so fearful. You didn't know where they were.

Different ones of our men hollered, "They're in the trees."

One of the guys who dug in with me started crying. Everytime he'd start crying, they'd open up on us with automatic weapons. I stuck my knife in his ribs and said, "I'm not getting killed for you. If you cry again I'm going to kill you because every time you start crying the gooks open up on us." I really meant it. I would have killed him that instant. He laid in the bottom of the hole then and whimpered quietly all night. Poor guy. But I wasn't going to let him get me killed.

That night I rubbed mud all over their faces. I'd already been in some combat, and it was apparent they hadn't.

The gooks started to crawl up on our hole. I saw them coming—or at least I thought I did. It was really black, but through the muzzle flashes and things like that, I saw this guy coming. I told the guys that were with me not to use their rifles at all because the muzzle flash would show them where we were. I slowly took a grenade from my belt, pulled the pin on it, let the spoon fly, held it as long as I dared, and then rolled it out on the top of our hole. I grabbed the guys by the head and yelled, "Get down!" It went off right in front of our hole. I think I killed a guy there.

It's weird, because sometimes you really don't know so much. A big part of the war was the suspense. If you killed one of the guys, they would risk a couple more to drag that person off so you wouldn't know if you killed him or not. After the battle we found gooks dead every place. They were under the leaves. Even some that were dying buried themselves so you wouldn't know, psychologically, if you had killed any of them or not.

It started getting light and all fury broke loose again. They were in the trees everywhere, and we mowed them down out of the trees. I shot one guy, and I kept shooting and shooting him because I thought he was still alive. Finally, I knocked him at least partially out of the tree. They'd tie themselves in with rags so that you wouldn't know if you killed them or not. It was really good psychological warfare, because you never really knew if you killed your enemy. We would shoot, but they took several of our men with them.

We then advanced up a ridge towards our main objective. I didn't know what the deal was, but we had to get there in a hurry. We fought our way foot by foot. It wasn't too serious. We kept pushing them back, and when we got to one area, there were big holes where our B-52's had dropped bombs.

We dug in and made overhead cover, and set up a perimeter there. We had just finished making camp when some young boys came toward camp. They were only about thirteen or fourteen years old. They had their old rifles over their heads hollering, "Choo Hoi," which means "I give up."

We weren't supposed to take any prisoners. I didn't have to shoot them—not that I wouldn't have. They just happened to be down a little bit from my hole. Suddenly I heard shots ring out and those kids fell like rag dolls. My stomach churned for a few moments, but then I rationalized they were probably planning on killing us. After all, General Sherman did say, "War is hell."

We dug in that night and built overhead cover. I set up two Claymore mines in front of my hole and waited. That night while I was pulling guard duty, I suddenly heard thud, thud, thud. I started screaming at the top of my lungs: "Incoming mortars, incoming mortars." The thud sound was them coming out of the tubes.

Everybody got up and scrambled in their holes. I was with some other guys in my hole, and there really wasn't room for me. I put the other guys in the hole, and I laid along side of it vertically so I'd have some protection.

The mortars were bursting all around us. It was a life-and-death situation. Some of our men did get killed. They were popping them like caps all around us. Then I heard the gooks coming. They always seemed to know everything we were doing.

They got in front of my position. I had two detonators (for the mines) in my hand as I laid next to the hole. I lit them both at once. It was dark, but they cleared up a mess of jungle out in front of us. I'm sure I killed some, but the next day we found blood but no bodies. They had drug them off. Somehow we got through the night. I heard some men crying and praying. I laughed and thought: *If I ever get out of here, I'm the one that will do it!*

Ahead of us—our artillery and planes started shelling and bombing. That sounded real good to us. The Special Forces were still ahead of us, perhaps a couple of miles away. I imagined they were all being killed with the artillery fire. They really pounded the hell out of it, and then we were ordered to move ahead.

There was a little sergeant who was a real coward. He should have been sent home because he couldn't help it. He was a nervous wreck. Everybody called him a coward. One of the officers said, "We'll teach him. We'll put him on point out front." I remember finding him on one side of a log—with two dead gooks on the other side of the log where they'd fought right down to the end. Guess you could say he was murdered.

As we took the area there was some fighting, but not much. The pounding of the big guns had either wiped them out or run them out of the area. I found a friend of mine that had been dragged by a bamboo rope around his neck, then hung, and then shot in the head. There were dead people every place—Americans and Vietnamese.

We set up a camp and were brought some hot chow—the first in days. We had been fighting maybe a week. By this time an entirely new set of hate entered us. The men would set up the Vietnamese bodies all around and stick cigarettes into their mouths. One lieutenant friend of mine who was really rebellious and slightly sick came running back waving a pair of ears—showing them to me. He said, "John, I know I got this S.O.B. No doubt about it. Want one?" He went to the 90-day wonder school, and was more like an enlisted man than an officer. He was F.O. (forward observer) and would call in the artillery. He had called in the artillery and felt that he was responsible for this guy's death so he had cut off his ears.

I had heard a lot of guys talk about taking ears, but I hadn't seen it until now. My head was spinning. *Harden up, Steer,* I told myself. *Hate the gooks, that's why you're here.* I felt crazy. Crazy. I thought it was funny how these dead gooks were all over.

Somebody had carved the 173d Airborne initials on one of the gook's forehead. I got up and stuck a cigarette I had lit up in a dead gook's lips. We ate the hot chow with dead stiffs propped up all over. It was funny and yet morbid. It was really sick, but in a few minutes it didn't bother us anymore. Routine, you know.

On this operation we went back the same way we came. The Special Forces were really happy that we got there.

As we were returning I saw this monkey and said, "Hey, man, that's a neat monkey."

One guy asked, "You want him?"

"Yeah," and right there I named him George—after my friend. They looked a lot alike, except my monkey was better looking. On the way back we were being picked up by helicopters. George, the monkey, just ate me up. He bit my fingers almost to ribbons so I held him by his throat. He'd never been in a helicopter before and was scared to death. I tried to give him to everybody, anybody.

"You want this thing? Take him."

"Heck, no, I don't want him." Nobody would take him. So I held him, almost choking him, trying to keep him from biting me. After that the monkey went with me on every airborne assault. He rode on my pack. He was a little spider monkey and got me in trouble at different times. He decided one day the C. O. papers were for litter. You can guess what the C. O. thought of that! From time to time we'd be smoking pot, and he'd smell it, so we would give him a joint. He'd fall out of trees all the way to the bottom branch and grab it with his tail or something. He would be out of his mind.

We were a strike force, and as a result were constantly on the move. The helicopter was the workhorse of the war. You could be fighting in one place and eight hours later be a hundred miles away.

Death became commonplace, and I constantly wondered, *Will it be me or my buddy this time?* Everything became more intense. Our madness and devil-take-care attitude seemed to increase. We lost about thirty men—two were blown into hamburger by two mines. They were carried out in plastic bags.

The first time I met George, he came in on a helicopter to replace somebody, fresh out of the States to the combat zone. George came over by me and I yelled, "Come on over here and stay in my hole tonight," (it was getting late) "then you don't have to dig a hole before you go to bed. You stay here with me."

He started crying. His mother had just been put in a mental institution. I couldn't deal with this kind of emotion. I absolutely could not deal with somebody crying. Right away I started hating him. Of course, I told him he was a baby and mocked him. Here this poor kid had just come in from the States, and had never seen anything like this. There were dead Americans shot up all over. People were running around like animals. Everything seemed to be a mess. Later we became the best of friends.

One time I was tromping through the jungle with diarrhea so bad I couldn't go a half hour without water running down my leg. You're wet. Your feet rot and chunks of meat are coming off. You would wake up with leaches in your nose, and any place else they decided to be. There were scorpions. There were snakes, mosquitoes, malaria, ringworm. There was bamboo poisoning on your arms, and they would be full of big blisters of pus. I mean big blisters of pus—not thin-skinned but big chunks of skin. You would take a stick and scrape them off as you gritted your teeth and watched the pus ooze out as you tried to wash it off.

I was bringing up the rear of the company. I thought I would die because of the dysentary. I stopped and tried to clean myself up, and when I started out again I had lost my men. I didn't know which direction they had gone. Here I was in enemy territory in the middle of Vietnam and I was lost. Let me tell you, I was scared.

Everyone seemed to pray a lot in Vietnam. I didn't know God, but I knew there was one. Boy, I prayed to Him a lot: "Help me" here and "Help me" there, and I believe He did! Now I was lost in the middle of the jungle. Finally I started going back on everything I'd learned on following, tracking, by watching for a broken blade of grass, twig, etc. I was supposed to be an experienced tracker. It wouldn't be hard to follow a hundred men, but the jungle was so thick and grown up. I was scared and knew any moment I would be ambushed. The enemy saw me, and I knew it. This was enemy territory. I might have been following them right into their base camp. Finally, two hours later, I caught up with my company. It was God because I didn't know if I was following the Vietnamese trail or ours!

Nobody had stopped to look for me. It was every man for himself most of the time. Later, in the same area, we came to an old Buddhist temple. Suddenly an old man came out with a shotgun and started shooting at us. Then he disappeared.

One of the men shouted, "Man, I can't go on. I cannot go another step. I'm worn-out." We were just pushed to go, go, go, and most of us felt just like that. So we left him there. I don't know if he ever caught up with us or not. If he didn't the Vietnamese killed him.

There were a couple of times when we had calls

for help on the radio—that Australians or Americans needed help—only to find it was the enemy trying to ambush us. As World War II had Tokyo Rose, we had Hanoi Hanna. At times during the night her voice could be heard over loud speakers the enemy had hidden. We would hear her over and over, saying, "G.I.'s go home. You can't win this war. Your wives are shacking up with the neighbor. Somebody else has your girl. You're going to get killed. Give up. Go home. Start rebelling against this war. Have you read the papers? All the Americans are protesting the war over here. Go home you G.I.'s." Man, it would make you think!

It was battle after battle, out and back, out and back. Then the word came: "We're moving up north." We had one more battle before being sent up north. We were going through the jungle and came upon this old French farmhouse. The Vietnamese had moved into it, but we ran them out and we moved in. We'd been in the jungle several weeks this time, pushing it, pressing and going. I was delirious and sick with high fever. I thought I had malaria.

After we got set up, I got an air mattress off a dead American. I hadn't had one for a long time, so this was really going to be a luxury sleeping on something other than mud. It was very important to me having this air mattress.

George came by and stepped on my air mattress. I screamed: "If you step on my air mattress again, I'll kill you." I was as serious as I could be. I would have killed him. Strange how much a piece of plastic could mean to a person.

He accepted the challenge. He wasn't one bit afraid of me. He walked right over and stepped on my air mattress again. To tell you the truth, I was sort of pleased because I didn't know George could fight. I thought he was a coward. He was no coward! He simply had some real emotions that he wasn't ashamed to hide. That's what I couldn't handle. I hid everything but my hate.

I threw a sandbag at him and knocked him down, and followed it up with both fists while he was on the ground. He was fighting back, and I mean fighting back, when one of our own men opened up with an M-60 machine gun over us. I mean that stopped us in a hurry. After that I had more respect for George than almost anyone I knew.

After all of that, I asked my platoon sergeant if I could go see the doctor because I was sick. He said, "Okay, Steer, but you had better not get out of the field, and don't try to pull any hanky-panky to get out of combat."

The doctor took one look at me and said, "Soldier, you have double pneumonia." He wired a big tag on me that said, "Dust off"—which meant I was to be on the next helicopter to the hospital. I was as pleased as could be. I went back and stuck the tag in my platoon sergeant's face. He cursed me every which way, and I simply smiled because I was so glad to get out of there.

While I got out, my company got hit really

hard, and many were killed. I was glad that I wasn't there in one sense. Yet in another sense, I was ashamed that I wasn't there to help fight.

At the hospital I talked a medic into giving me a lot of codeine. I stayed stoned for two days. I might have thought for a day or two I was out of the war, but I wasn't. My third day in the hospital we got mortared. They wiped out a lot of our Air Force, which was unusual. Usually the Air Force didn't get involved, but they got close enough with their mortars to put them right in the barracks.

I had to help carry the wounded guys that were in the hospital down into the underground shelter. Then after they quit mortaring, carry them back up into the hospital. We weren't hit, but all around us was hit real bad.

Soon it was back to the field. Back to the same old stuff—humping the boonies, we called it. You just go and go and go. The fatigue at times almost overwhelmed us, and we wouldn't always think straight. During one of our little battles several of us shot at the same gook. I was certain that it was my bullet that got him. After we killed him, I went over to the body and kicked off his hat—about three feet of hair fell out. We had killed a sixteen-year-old girl. I felt kind of rotten over that, but she would have killed me, because she had a machine gun and was out to kill.

Back from the hospital the word came: "We're going up north, and they don't play up there." Everybody was saying, "They don't play up

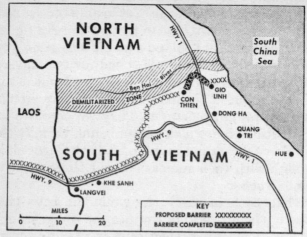

KEY

PROPOSED BARRIER XXXXXXXXX

BARRIER COMPLETED XXXXXXXXX

AREA OF MAP AT RIGHT

north. It's a whole different ball game from what we have been doing. Now we are going into the actual war. When we go up north—there's not going to be many to come back." We didn't believe them and thought, *Right. Right. They're just psyching us up.*

Our entire battalion was flown to Dak To. In the meantime, I had gotten rid of my monkey, George. He had gotten mean and was too much trouble. I gave him to an Air Force guy who asked, "What do I feed him?"

"Man, you don't have to feed him. He'll steal anything he wants. Just give him a little marijuana once in a while, and he'll be all right."

By this time I was smoking dope. When I first got to Nam I didn't because I thought everybody was a dopehead. I drank if I could get it, but you couldn't get booze, only very rarely, but you could get pot any place. They had marijuana everywhere. After seeing a few things that I'd seen, I was glad to smoke some once in a while to forget. They're talking these days of legalizing it here in the States. The stuff will make you go crazy. I saw a guy lay on top of the bunker while mortars were blowing everything apart. He said they were so pretty that he laid on top of the bunker and watched them all night. We weren't all dopers in my outfit. Maybe we would smoke a joint once in a while, but there were only a couple of guys in my outfit that were really dopers.

We knew the next morning we would move out. There was a "hippy" soldier kid that came and sat by me. He really was a sweet kid. To him everything was "Cool, man." He was a good fighter and cool when he was out there. He showed me photos of his mother and dad. I almost felt a part of his family. Harvey really loved his family.

The next morning word was passed down that we were going to travel on the trail. We had never done that because it was suicide with all the ambushes that were set up by the gooks. As we walked I found twisted bamboo along the road. There were other signs also, but the lieutenant just ignored them. As we continued down the trail, we started hearing gunfire. I was about in the center of the file when we heard this fire. I was experienced and a pretty good soldier. I told the guys behind me: "Split and get off this thing."

Again I said, "Spread out and get off the trail." Then it came back—this was simply recon by fire—our own men were shooting into suspicious-looking areas trying to draw fire. I didn't believe it, but we were ordered to go on so we kept moving. There was more firing. The lieutenant said, "Recon by fire. Keep going."

I knew better than that. I could hear the AK-47's, the Chinese guns. I was familiar with the different kinds of weapons by this time. I knew the sound of the Viet Cong weapons that were being fired. They were not American, and I knew it. You couldn't see anything because it was a narrow trail. We were stretched out probably a half mile.

The lieutenant again passes down: "Keep coming. Keep coming."

Man, I thought it was stupid, but we were under orders and kept going. As a result he walked us right smack dab into an ambush. He was probably thinking about the glory of what we were about to do, looking for contact, and found it. Instead of using his head and having us fall back and set up a perimeter, or sending out search and destroy squads and setting up ambushes for them, around them, he marched us right into them.

Guys were getting slaughtered, but we kept going, and going and going. Now we set up a simulation of a perimeter (about forty acres) around this hill. I was in weapons platoon so I was in the center of the perimeter. They wouldn't let us mortar, and that really ticked me off. They were afraid that we'd get too many air bursts hitting our own people.

The battle continued, and I was helping with plasma and cutting down some trees. Finally they called up for an ammo bearer for the machine gunners. I took the box of ammunition down a real steep, slimy hill. Bullets hit all around me on my way down. I was scared! I got down there and saw a lot of guys already shot up. It was a mess.

Coming down the hill I could see the enemy running around where I couldn't see them when I was down there because I was level with them. I was wanting to get out of there. Somebody yelled, "Steer, so and so is wounded. Take him with you. Carry him out of here."

I threw the guy over my shoulder and went back up that slimy, slippery hill, exposed. Bullets were hitting all around me. At one point the guy I was carrying got shot again. When I got to the top I was still petrified. I'd purposed in my heart that I was not going back down that hill again because it was suicide. Then I got busy, and stayed busy so I wouldn't be sent back down there.

We had to cut a lot of bamboo down so that the helicopters could come in and get the wounded out of there. One of my friends was shot four times in the guts, and I kept lighting him a cigarette—one after another. I hope he's alive today. He might have made it. I never knew.

There was one guy who was so frightened that when he got shot through the hand he went into shock and died.

They called for an ammo bearer again.

Harvey, the hippy that I made friends with the night before, went down. I felt like I should have gone, but they didn't say "Steer," and I'd already been down there once. If I could keep from it, I wasn't going again.

Harvey went down. About that time some American gun ships came in with the helicopters with machine guns on them—6,000 rounds per minute. Somehow Harvey was in the way when they came through and they ripped him in half. He was killed by American gunfire. I really took on. I thought I would die from guilt. I took on the spirit of suicide and guilt. I was different from then on. Now I had to be first. I had to be up front. I had to be! I had to be!

The rest of the story is that we got wiped out. The gooks ran a human wave attack over the wounded. They tortured some of them, and the rest they shot in the head. There were about eighty men shot in the head. I saw the mess, but not the slaughter. We heard some guys screaming, "Oh, God, they're shooting them in the head. Oh, God, there is nothing we can do. There is nothing we can do."

The lieutenant was in the hole with his radioman, scared to death. I hated this radioman because he had shot a friend of mine in the leg. They were the ones that had gotten us into it. Now I was hurt and hateful. I was wondering whether I was ever going to get off the hill alive because there were less and less of us left. Yet the enemy was still fighting. But because I hadn't been shot (most of the guys that lived had been shot), I was still in good shape, so it was just common sense for me to continue to fight longer than the rest.

I was one of the last ones on the last helicopter off the hill. It was fearful, but part of me wanted to be the last one. Part of me wanted to get killed because I felt so ashamed that my friends were killed and I wasn't.

Our battle was in view of Dak To, where there were thousands of men. This was up in the mountains. They could see the smoke. They could hear the shooting. It was maybe two miles away, but there was nothing they could do either. They couldn't get dropped in there by helicopters because there was no place to land. They couldn't have forced marched there because the jungle was so thick.

WAKE UP AMERICA

Wake up America, you don't even know you're asleep,
You sent men off to a distant land, your honor for to
    keep,
Fifty-eight thousand fought and died, but all were not
    brought home,
Won't you accept responsibility and help us set them
    free?

Many have died from Agent Orange, the cancer tells the
    tale,
Others suffer from Post Traumatic Stress, wonder why
    they end up in jail,
Wake up America, you don't even know you're asleep,
You sent men off to a distant land, your honor for
    to keep.

In training we never heard the word defeat, we were
    willing to give all,
We fought beside men, brave and true, watched many a
    a comrade fall,
You tied our hands, you lost the war, then we received
    the blame,
Don't you owe us anything? We suffered in your name.

Wake up America, you don't even know you're
    asleep,
You sent men off to a distant land, your honor for to
    keep.

Poem
by
John Steer

6
DAK TO

Back at Dak To we lined up the packs because that was all that was left of most of our friends—the packs. We went through them, found pictures of their families, and got the good food that was left. If they had a good knife we stole it, but the personal stuff like the pictures and letters, we were sorting them out so they could be sent home to their folks. It was like a nightmare.

They brought in some people to write a book about us. I don't know if it ever got written, but I know that my name was one of the few that was left. I personally talked to Westmoreland a couple of times.   Once he talked to us sitting on the hood of his jeep.   He told us many times that we were the toughest in the army, and that he was proud of us. One hundred and thirty of us had just kicked the h--- out of five to eight hundred Vietnamese.

I felt like spitting in his face, yet the *esprit de corps* (pride) was so strong. I was proud that here's the General of Vietnam talking to a handful of us personally, and patting us on the back. In our guts we knew it was all a facade, a big joke. Yet, you're putting on this show. It was crazy. The whole thing was crazy. I was so full of hate for the Vietnamese. I just hated them with a passion—all of them!

There were just a few of us left. They roped us off. We could stay in a certain area. The rest of the army, LEGS and different outfits were stationed all around us, but we were in the center there just like a bunch of freaks. They said they were going to send what was left of us the next day to pick up our buddies in rubber bags. We had already seen some of them picked up in rubber bags and helped. I saw one guy's head roll off the helicopter as it took off. The bag came open, and the head rolled out. They had to throw the head back onto the chopper. I don't think that we could have taken it to go back up there with these guys that we had fought with for four and a half months—friends of ours that we had lived with—and then pick up their pieces and put them in rubber bags. That is what the orders were. We were to go the next day. Thank God, somebody had enough sense that they changed the orders and they sent up another company.

I was at the point now I just didn't give a d— about anything. I had a tooth that was abscessed. I had dirty fatigues. They hadn't even gotten us clean fatigues yet. I was bloody, dirty, and I got on a helicopter. Technically, I went AWOL.

"Where are you going?" I asked the pilot. He said, "Da Nang." It was on the Red China Sea. He broke the law. I broke the law, but I went with him. I couldn't have gotten on base any other way. I came in on this helicopter. I guess I was about half crazy literally, maybe more.

I got off the helicopter at Da Nang and went to the NCO club. I found it, and could not believe this. Here, not very many miles away—we're living like animals, sleeping in the jungle and just crazy—and I come here and the guys are wearing suits. It's just like in the States. Psychologically I couldn't handle it.

Inside the club they asked, "Who are you? Where do you think you're going?"

"I'm coming in here, and I'm getting drunk out of my skull," I answered.

"Man, you can't come in here," one man said and physically stopped me. I was ready to fight.

Some older sergeants were at a table (they were mostly Air Force guys). They came over and asked, "What's going on?"

"This guy thinks he's coming in here."

I had blood all down the front of my shirt from carrying wounded guys and dead guys. I stunk. I had long hair and hadn't shaved in three, four, or five days.

These sergeants asked, "Did you just return from the battle at Dak To?"

I replied, 'Yeah, I did, and I am real lucky to be here." They took me and bought me all the booze I could drink. They took me home afterwards, and I got a shower. I hadn't had a shower in I don't know how long. Hot water! It was like heaven must be, I thought. I couldn't believe it because the showers that I had had were out of a little canvas bag hung up in a tree so you get about a gallon and a half of water.

I still had bamboo poisoning all over my arms. They got me to one of their dentists who fixed up my tooth. Man, I was getting cleaned up, getting better. I was treating the ringworm with the shoe powder. I stayed there a couple of days—staying drunk. These guys really helped me. Technically they were aiding and abetting somebody that had run off.

I went swimming every day in the Red China Sea. It was so beautiful. There was a fence that went out a long way into the sea. We stayed on one side of the fence. You could see the fishing boats and everything not too far on the other side. "What is that over there?" I asked.

"That's a Vietnamese village. We slip over there sometimes and get a little," I was told.

I thought that sounded good. That night I went out of the American compound on my belly through the barbed wire. I got over there to the little whorehouse and a bar. I spent the night with a gal. I crawled back through the American wires before morning. Come to find out, the next day they towed an American Jeep out of that village—it was riddled with bullets and had three corpses lying in the back. The village was full of North Vietnamese soldiers. It was fenced off from the base, but it was like it was on the base. Once again I had been spared.

From there it was kind of funny. I got to feeling guilty. My men are back there in the field. I'm here. I'm getting my sanity back. So I got on another helicopter—I don't know how I did it or what I did. I talked to different people and they got me on a helicopter that was going back to Dak To. I got back there and simply walked over to my men.

New guys had come in now. They were all brand new men, and said, "Hey, man, don't worry about it. We'll show you what's going on." They'd been in the country like a week. They were patting me on the back and saying, "It will be all right. We know what's going on. Just stick with us. We'll show you." They didn't know that I'd been in the country five months already. I never told them, but soon they found that I was one of the men that was left from the last hill and they felt foolish. Everything was so disorganized that nobody knew I had been gone. I could have been a Russian spy I guess! I didn't have any identification except my Geneva Convention card.

I couldn't believe it, but I was afraid to go back out there. I had it in my heart to get revenge—but I also wanted to live to get home.

They needed a cook at Dak To. I talked to somebody about the job of cooking. It was disgraceful for me to do this because I was an infantry paratrooper. Nobody blamed me, however, because I'd seen more combat and lived through it longer than most of them. By now I had received one Purple Heart, and turned one down. Some of the guys were already cracking up, going crazy. A couple of guys even killed themselves. I went over to the cook shack and worked there all day. In the meantime they were getting a new company ready to move out.

The mess shack was a nightmare. The other cooks were all stoned and had acid rock music blaring in their ears. I couldn't handle it and went back to my men. So the day I could have been resting, getting ready to go out, I worked cooking.

By this time I had the respect of most of the men. They knew that I had been around a long time. Even the lieutenants were coming to me and asking me stuff. Not because I was so smart, but because I had lived longer than most. Boy, did we lose lieutenants. We just couldn't keep them alive. They were dumb. They had only been through 90-day wonder school and, after all, they were just kids like the rest of us.

We moved back out again. It was just one battle after another. One guy broke his back when he fell down a mountain that we were climbing. One of our men got a letter from his wife that she was going to leave him. He went over to his hole crying. There were three or four men standing in the hole writing letters. One of the guys cursed him—which is really common when you fight like we did. He told these guys they had better shut up, or he'd kill them.

The next thing we knew there was an explosion. I was only about 100 feet from it. This guy had jumped in the hole with his buddies and pulled the pin on a grenade. These were his friends. One guy lived through it. This was all over a "Dear John" letter, but it wasn't just that but the tension, the pressure, the curse of Vietnam.

One of our men ran into the enemy screaming, "I can't take it anymore. I can't take it anymore." He went nuts, and the enemy took care of the rest. There was another guy we had to tie up at nights. We couldn't get any helicopters in, and at night he'd go bananas and try to kill us. They kept him tied up in front of the C. O.'s tent at night. I don't know whatever happened to him.

We lived on the constant brink of insanity. Most of us were always this way—always borderline crazy, and afraid that you were going to go over. By this time all I wanted to do was kill the enemy. Boy, how I wanted to kill them. If somebody killed one and I didn't that day, I really felt bad, jealous.

One day we moved into an area that had been pounded with B-52's I suppose. There was very little contact, but there were gooks wandering around out there, all spaced-out from the concussion. This one friend of mine that was really a crazy and messed me up later, killed two Vietnamese this day. I was really upset because I hadn't even seen one. It had become almost like deer hunting to me.

One time a guy yelled, "There's one."

"Wait a minute. Wait for me," I yelled. I didn't want them to shoot until I got in on it too. There was a Vietnamese officer wandering around in shell shock and the three of us shot him all at once. It felt good. It really did. When you kill somebody, it's so final. It's done, and there's nothing else you can do. It's just done! I was just filled with insane hate.

We didn't have much contact for several months, but they pushed us so hard. We'd go day and night, day and night, moving. We'd move all day. We'd start out before light. Then we'd move until dark and dig a hole after dark and build an overhead cover on it, because we usually got mortared at night. The Vietnamese always seemed to know where we were.

We'd set up a perimeter at night and set our trip flares out in front. A couple of times they'd hit the trip flare and light up the area. Usually by the time you'd see them, get your gun, and get the Claymore detonator in your hand, they'd be gone. They'd sneak in like that and blow your brains out. You'd be sitting there trying to hide your cigarette. If they saw the glow of your cigarette, you would be one dead soldier.

7
HILL 875

Then came the big battle on November 19, 1967, on hill 875. We'd taken another hill before this, and we lost several men. We even lost our company commander so we had some more new people. This was another thing to deal with. We always had new people because if some got wounded bad enough or killed, they sent a replacement. They didn't know what they were doing. These guys were supposed to be protecting your butt, and you never knew what they were doing. It takes experience to learn. If they live long enough, they learn. If they don't, they die.

We were told ahead of time that we were going to take the hill. I believe the hill had already been taken by the marines, and then was taken back by the enemy. We were told that we were going to take it. It was going to be a bloody battle, and most of our men would be lost taking it. I say "hill" but it was more like hills in a mountainous area, and it was thick jungle. It wasn't

too thick going up the hill because it had already been bombed. They had pounded it, but the gooks had been there so long in base camp they had lots of overhead cover and you couldn't hurt them. Now when they said, "There are not going to be many of you come back," we knew they meant it.

We were asking, "Why? This is stupid. Why are we doing this?" But you know—God and country—and still revenge, crazy, hateful revenge. By this time I really didn't believe I was going to get out of this alive. I had seen so many people killed. There was always that hope: maybe I won't get shot, but it wasn't much of a hope, and my hope continued to deteriorate.

I'd see friends of mine around the same area that were supposed to be taken out of the field by helicopter. You're supposed to be taken out a couple of days before you go back to the States after your year is up. They wouldn't send a helicopter out there for one man, and that night he'd get killed. I remember one really nice guy. He'd dig deep holes because it was getting close to his time to be going home. He should have been out of the field a week already, and he got killed. Then you'd wonder: does anybody get to go home out of this God-forsaken place? Some did, of course, and oh, they would be so happy. I would be happy to go home too!

Then the battle started. We started up the hill. "A" Company was famous by this time amongst the circles over there. We had a bounty on our heads. This time we didn't have to spearhead it.

There were three companies ahead of us. They went first. We were going up this hill. It was pretty steep. They engaged in contact. Then it was like every man for himself. We were hollering and screaming and charging the hill. We were psyched up that we were going to take it.

They kept moving us down. Finally we got what I thought was the hill, but apparently according to the papers, it was only a plateau, or "a hill," but not "the hill." We fought our way up and lost a lot of men. We set up a perimeter on top, and the men began to dig in. We're fighting against thousands of Vietnamese, and there's only about 400 of us. They're dug in on the top of a hill, and we're climbing up the hill—wide open targets. They mowed a lot of us down. We fought like crazy. A lot of guys had been killed, and many more had been wounded.

This time more gooks had come in behind us. We were surrounded. The orders were for "A" Company to go back down the hill and cut a landing zone. It was too hot up here. I never did understand their strategy, but apparently they knew what they were doing, so we fought our way back down the hill. We had just fought our way up the hill, now we had to expose ourselves again and fight our way back down the hill. Crazy, but everything in Nam seemed crazy. We got down the hill, and we set up another perimeter, a small one—this time company size. There were maybe seventy left out of the company of over 100.

Intelligence got it that the gooks were bringing up another regiment to our rear on the Ho Chi Minh Trail. I said I would volunteer to go back down the trail until we made contact—trying to slow them down or something.

Me, Lazuava and another boy—I don't even care to mention him because it was because of him we got shot up. He was afraid. Lots of people are afraid, and there are times that I was afraid. I mean this guy talked like he was John Wayne all the time, but when the real stuff hit he'd be the one following me around trying to get a medal or something. I didn't care about any medal. I didn't want any. I hated the sight of medals. To this day, I don't know what I would do if I met this guy again. When I got my first purple heart I told them I didn't want it. I didn't take it because I didn't go over there seeking medals. I just wanted to kill the gooks and get home with my life.

The three of us went down the trail. We're maybe a quarter of a mile away from our company in enemy territory. This other guy had on a new radio helmet. We set up a little ambush with Lazuava's machine gun. I was going to help him with the machine gun. He was also my squad leader. I respected him because he'd been in a lot of combat. We set up the machine gun and waited. All the time there is firing going on. There's a lot of big battles going on—maybe a half mile away, and we could hear them.

Pretty soon here they come. One guy got real close to me. Lazuava was screaming: "Kill that guy, kill him!" The machine gun was jammed. I couldn't see him. I could not see the guy! I was trembling. I had my gun and was looking—looking all over. I couldn't see him. He was only thirty steps in front of me and on an open road! I guess it was the excitement and his camouflage. He was lying in the road. Then I saw him and put twenty rounds in him and splattered him all over the road.

I snapped another clip in my gun and said, "Lazuava, cover me. I'm going across the trail. Then I'll cover you and you can come across. We've got to find a way back to our company now because if we wait another minute we're going to really be in trouble." We were in trouble, and we didn't realize how bad.

I ran across the trail, and as I did I sprayed a whole round of ammunition, and he covered me with the machine gun. I snapped another clip in and said, "Okay, NOW!" He ran across while I sprayed several rounds, and he got across. He was right next to me. I cursed him because I was lower than he was. I said, "Lazuava, get your butt down." Just as I grabbed him I hollered, "I'm hit!" With the same two rounds that got me in the back they took off his head.

I looked in disbelief and cried, "Lazuava, Lazuava. Oh, my God, no." I always thought maybe I should have stayed and tried to take his pulse or something, but I knew he was dead. Again the guilt was there: Why him and not me?

His machine gun dropped to the ground. By now there were more of them coming, flanking us. They kept coming—I knew there were hundreds behind them. The only thing they had to shoot at so far was us, and that's because our position was exposed when the guy with the radio helmet saw them, got scared and ran. There were bullets going everywhere. The guy who ran didn't get killed, but if you can believe it—got a silver star.

---

the hill and Alpha started work on the helicopter landing zone, 2nd Battalion's "trouble" began.

North Vietnamese troops opened fire. Snipers blazed away from treetops. Mortar shells crunched into the hillside.

Pfc. Ernest Lazuava, 20, New York City, posted with other troopers around the zone, fired into the jungle, at first not seeing anything to shoot at.

Then about 100 North Vietnamese—"a whole hill full of them"—charged out of the bamboo less than 10 feet from where Lazuava and James Kelly, 19, Fort Myers, Fla., were patrolling.

THE TWO soldiers fired back, then sprinted for the safety of defenses their buddies had thrown up round the landing zone.

The first mortar round killed Alpha Company's commander, two radio operators and all the unit's medics.

The survivors picked up the wounded and, guns blazing, tried to break out and link up with Charlie and Delta companies up the hill.

Lazuava stayed behind to hold off the charging North Vietnamese, ignoring the pleas of Kelly, who never will forget that moment.

"I kept yelling to him: 'Pull back! Pull back!'" Kelly remembers. "He just wouldn't do it.

The young Puerto Rican kept firing as North Vietnamese bullets ripped into his body. Finally, Lazuava's rifle emptied and he fell dead.

First Lt. Joseph Sheridan, 24, Orlando, Fla., who took command of Alpha Company, remembers Lazuava.

"IF IT HADN'T been for him, most of us wouldn't have made it." Sheridan said.

I had to get out of there so I made a run for it. I was hit in the back and didn't know how bad. I thought I was going to die. I looked back and here is my whole back laid open. You don't realize how God has put us together and that skin is stretched over your back. Well, it just laid right across my collarbone, one came out my arm, one came out of the top of my shoulder. It's like somebody took a scalpel and laid my skin open to the bone. I didn't know if there were holes through me or what. I couldn't see. I was scared.

I started crawling back to my company as fast as I could. Now I could see the gooks. They were shooting at me. I actually crawled between them because they were fifty yards apart. I was scared and trembling, not because of myself, but because of Lazuava. He was my buddy, and he was gone, gone forever! Here we go again, one or two friends that I've got left in the whole lousy company, and Lazuava got it.

I was going as fast as I could. If I had felt better I would have killed him then and there. Like I said, he got a silver star for getting Lazuava killed, and me shot in the back. Anyway, I got back to the company.

I talked to the lieutenant, or whoever was left in charge, saying, "We've got to get back with the battalion because they're going to walk over us like ants."

"No, we'll stay," he answered.

"The h— we will." And I started pointing guns at them saying, "Get going." I started giv ing orders around there. It wasn't my job, but that's what I was doing anyway. I knew we were all dead if I didn't. We had to fight our way back up to the top with the battalion to have any chance of making it.

One guy was wounded but far from dead. He said, "Man, I can't go." I stuck a gun in him and said, "You're a dead man if you don't. We're taking that hill again, right now!"

The whole time the enemy was still fighting. Guys are dropping every place. So what was left of our company I didn't know, but I know I was giving the orders and we took the hill again. We lost more men on the way up. I dragged some of them, tried to carry them, pushed them, threatened to kill them because a lot of guys were ready to give up. Many of them had been shot already, but so had I. I was scared, but I wasn't going to let those gooks kill them.

What was left of the company got back up to the top of the hill. There were maybe half of the company left. I started playing like John Wayne. I could see the fear in the people. They had a right to be afraid. We were fighting for life and were we outnumbered! I don't know how many to one.

The gooks seemed like they didn't care whether they lived or died. They human wave attacked you. You'd hear the bugles play, screams, bonzi yells, then they'd come. It was kill as many of them as you could, and try to push them back. Then they'd come again.

I went around from hole to hole encouraging

the men. This wasn't my job. I was no officer. I was the "acting jack" sergeant because those allocations hadn't come down to make me a hard sergeant. I wasn't with my weapons platoon anymore. It's interesting thinking about it—the decisions that I made were decisions concerning people's lives. It wasn't my job, but someone had to do it.

I'm certain we left a lot of wounded behind. I never stopped to go around all the bushes where the guys were shot to see whether they were still breathing or not. We'd have to keep moving if any of us at all were going to make it. I guess that's why I went crazy and threatened to kill anybody that disobeyed what I told them to do.

I finally got so exhausted I simply couldn't go anymore. I had lost a lot of blood. I sat down under a tree. I saw a rocket grenade hit real close—it got a friend of mine. There was no safe place. I could see it all happening, but I couldn't believe it was happening to me. It was all so bizarre. It was like I was trying to get killed. Every time I'd do something more dangerous here I was the one that was left. It just didn't make sense. My friends, Maynard, Lazuava and Shoop, were lost in this battle. I knew other guys, but I couldn't remember them. They weren't close to me like others.

While I was shooting, a bullet hit my gun' forearm. It shattered and knocked the gun out of my hands. I got another gun. You didn't have to go far, they were all over the place.

Ammunition was dropped by parachute. I

was outside the perimeter. I guess some brave men had to go out there and get it. I was too weak. They could only bring in an armload at a time. Several of them got killed trying to get it. There weren't too many of us that expected to get off that hill alive. I didn't. I was going to kill every S.O.B. there that I could. How I hated!

They just kept picking us off. I don't know what the officers were doing, or if they were even alive. I imagine by this time plans were already going on to bring some more help. When darkness came upon the battlefield our airmen were going to drop parachute flares on the enemy. However, they dropped them right smack dab in the middle of our perimeter. They lit us up like a Christmas tree—so the gooks had something to shoot at. It was just another in a line of stupid mistakes.

When that happened, I laid down with a half a poncho over me. I was close to Father Waters, and he was praying and giving plasma. He jumped in a hole one time and killed a couple of gooks after they killed the machine gunner. He became my friend. He'd say mass in the jungle while the men would sit on helmets. During mass if a sniper or someone would open up on us (you know mass takes about ten minutes), he'd sometimes quickly say, "Mass is ended. Get out of here!" He was quite a guy. I've always hoped in my heart that he was a Christian. I sure wasn't one then. I know one thing, Father Waters was a man.

I continued to lay there and saw how they

were shooting at everybody. There was no way to shoot them. We couldn't see them, but they could sure see us. Apparently these parachute flares were more than just to light up the enemy. They were a marker for the F-100's to drop their bombs. So some phantom jets came in and dropped a 750-pound bomb right in the middle of our perimeter—right where all the wounded and casualties were. Suddenly everything went blank.

I do not know how long I was out, but suddenly even before I could open my eyes, I sensed I was dead. *Oh, God, I bet I'm in hell!* I thought. The pain was pulsating through my entire body. I slowly opened my eyes and there were arms, legs, heads, and bodies everywhere. I realized I had been thrown a long distance from where I was hiding under the poncho. I could now feel the blood oozing from my mouth, nose and ears from the concussion of the bomb's blast. I started swallowing the blood like a starving man. I wanted to keep it in me, somehow thinking it would help keep me alive. I swallowed as fast as I could.

Then I heard screams of the dying all around me. *I have got to keep my eyes open and try to see what's going on,* I thought. I lifted my right arm to wipe away the blood, but I couldn't feel my hand touch my face. Like a bolt of lightening I thrust my eyes open and saw a bloody, ragged stump where my arm had been. "Oh, God," I cried, "my arm has been blown off."

My right leg was just hanging it seemed by a

few sinews and some skin. "My body, my body," I cried, "I'm half a man." Then instinctively I knew I was going to die. I had no impression whatsoever that I would live. My blood was quickly being drained from my body. Soon I would be another Vietnam statistic. **John Steer dies in battle.** I could see it listed in our local papers.

I thought, *What will Mom and Dad think? I love both of them so much and never was able to really tell them. Oh, Dad, I really do love you.* Then I heard myself cry out: "God, don't let me go to hell!" It was as loud as I could scream. Again I cried out, "God, don't let me go to hell."

I really hadn't been taught much about hell. I'd been taught some stupid junk, for example: all Catholics go to hell, and all protestants go to heaven. I had learned things like: we don't make the sign of the cross because Catholics do. Let me tell you, that stuff doesn't help when you are thousands of miles from home on a forsaken battlefield crying. I had taken two years of catechism, but I never grasped why Jesus died on the cross. I thought God was awful stupid to put His Son on the cross. But somehow I knew right then if I died I was going to the devil's hell. I knew it! I knew I deserved it. I knew that was where I belonged. Again I screamed, "God, don't let me go to hell."

I passed out, and when I woke up again all my bleeding had stopped. My mouth was clean. My right arm stump was dry. My right leg, even where I was shot in the back was no longer bleeding. I thanked God and cried. Somehow I knew God was alive. I cried aloud, "God, I'm going to live. I'm really going to live." I knew instantly that God had heard a sin-sick and dying soldier's cry.

The gooks were going around slaughtering guys, shooting them in the head. I heard guys screaming as they were being dismembered. I called, "Somebody come and get me!" then I realized I had better shut up—there was no one around but the gooks. Still I knew I was going to live. I had met God. I *KNEW* I had met God!

My left arm—I hadn't used it for a day and a half. Now I could use it because I had to. I didn't have the right one. I began to crawl to a better hiding place. I really don't know how far. I found some thick underbrush and hid there. There were two dead soldiers lying near so I pulled these guys over the top of me. I drank one of their canteens of water. I laid there with these Americans on top of me—hoping that the gooks wouldn't find and kill me.

8
BEING PUT BACK TOGETHER

I watched the sun come, and then the moon came up. Then the sun came up. I don't know how long I laid there. I think it was at least two days. I was in and out of consciousness. It seemed my entire life was before me. I thought and thought and thought. I wondered if my dad cared about me. I hoped so. I caused him so much trouble and been such a bum. *Does anyone care? Is anyone praying for me? Dad, please care.*

The loneliness of those hours was almost more than I could bear. The moments that I was conscious I did a lot of "foxhole" talking with God. I promised, "God, I'll go to Sunday school, and any other religious things You want me to do." I didn't know about being born again, but I knew there was a God, and He was keeping me alive.

The third day another battalion had fought their way in to us. When they saw what had happened (some of them had just come from the

States), they got sick and started vomiting and crying. American men, stinking from the rotten flesh, were lying there covered with flies. The fire of the bomb had burned a lot of people. You could smell the flesh still smouldering.

When I realized they were our guys I screamed for help. One of the guys said to me, "Man, don't worry. You're going to be all right." When they found me with the decaying men on top of me, some grossed out. "They'll put your arm back on. Don't worry about your arm. They'll put that on."

I said, "You're a liar. There isn't any way they're going to put that arm back on. Give me some of that morphine." Quickly they gave me a shot of morphine. We usually carried it on us, but had used it all up.

Then they tried to move me. "Oh, God," I screamed out. The morphine didn't do any good, and the pain was more than I could bear. I was really cut up. I felt sorry for these guys for what they had to do and see.

I was told later that the first two helicopters they tried to bring in were shot down. I was the first to get out of there because I was in a very critical condition. They brought in the third helicopter. There was shooting going on all over the place. They wrapped me in a poncho and grabbed me like a sack of potatoes. They wouldn't land the helicopter because it was too dangerous, so they had to throw me about six feet up into the helicopter.

The helicopter took off like a bullet. When it

got high you could see the gooks shooting at us. There was a medic there that never got off the helicopter, but he was running back and forth with an M-16, plus there were two door gunners with M-60 machine guns. This medic went bananas and stepped two or three times on what was left of my arm. I ripped the poncho off with my left arm and let him see the stump he was stepping on. I told him if he stepped on it again I'd kill him. Here I was getting out of the field—I should have been happy—and I'm still wanting to kill people—my own people!

Later I got a letter from Japan saying that they took six hits on the helicopter. I was so mad because the pilot wanted me to put him in for a medal. I didn't care about medals. I never answered his letter, but I used to tell people, "Give the medals to the guys that are dead. They're the ones that deserve them." They deserved them, I'm sure, because all of these other guys were getting killed. But at the time I was so bitter, I couldn't think about anybody getting a medal in order to save somebody's life. A lot of men wouldn't fly into a hot zone like that, and it was a real hero who flew me out. You couldn't really blame them. After all, six were shot down before him. Yet, he flew one in for me.

They took me to a tent hospital not very far away. As soon as the doctor came to me I asked, "Doc, you're not going to try to put that arm back on?"

"My God, no. Son, you already have gangrene," he answered.

"Am I going to live?"

"Yes, you're going to live. Don't worry about it."

Since then I have found many doctors (thank God, not all) don't know how to deal with death. They'll lie to you instead of telling you that you might be burning in hell fire in twenty minutes.

The doctor did absolutely nothing for me. He wrapped me in a bandage from my feet to my neck like a mummy. That was all he did, and he put me on a big helicopter to the main hospital. When they got me off the helicopter, they had to put me in an ambulance to take me the rest of the way. I'd left first, but I didn't get treated

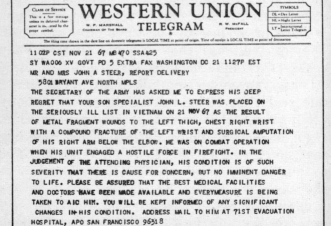

CLASS OF SERVICE

This is a fast message unless its deferred character is indicated by the proper symbol.

WESTERN UNION

W. P. MARSHALL
CHAIRMAN OF THE BOARD

TELEGRAM

R. W. McFALL
PRESIDENT

SYMBOLS

DL = Day Letter
NL = Night Letter
LT = International Letter Telegram

The filing time shown in the date line on domestic telegrams is LOCAL TIME at point of origin. Time of receipt is LOCAL TIME at point of destination

11 02P CST NOV 21 67 MB 470 SSA425

SY WA006 XV GOVT PD 5 EXTRA FAX WASHINGTON DC 21 1127P EST

MR AND MRS JOHN A STEER, REPORT DELIVERY

5801 BRYANT AVE NORTH MPLS

THE SECRETARY OF THE ARMY HAS ASKED ME TO EXPRESS HIS DEEP
REGRET THAT YOUR SON SPECIALIST JOHN L. STEER WAS PLACED ON
THE SERIOUSLY ILL LIST IN VIETNAM ON 21 NOV 67 AS THE RESULT
OF METAL FRAGMENT WOUNDS TO THE LEFT THIGH, CHEST RIGHT WRIST
WITH A COMPOUND FRACTURE OF THE LEFT WRIST AND SURGICAL AMPUTATION
OF HIS RIGHT ARM BELOW THE ELBOW. HE WAS ON COMBAT OPERATION
WHEN HIS UNIT ENGAGED A HOSTILE FORCE IN FIREFIGHT. IN THE
JUDGEMENT OF THE ATTENDING PHYSICIAN, HIS CONDITION IS OF SUCH
SEVERITY THAT THERE IS CAUSE FOR CONCERN, BUT NO IMMINENT DANGER
TO LIFE. PLEASE BE ASSURED THAT THE BEST MEDICAL FACILITIES
AND DOCTORS HAVE BEEN MADE AVAILABLE AND EVERYMEASURE IS BEING
TAKEN TO AID HIM. YOU WILL BE KEPT INFORMED OF ANY SIGNIFICANT
CHANGES IN HIS CONDITION. ADDRESS MAIL TO HIM AT 71ST EVACUATION
HOSPITAL, APO SAN FRANCISCO 96318

KENNETH G WICKHAM MAJOR GENERAL USA THE ADJUTANT GENERAL

first because a lot of these guys were there ahead of me. They hadn't stopped at the tent.

They put me on a shelf. I used to think they did it just to see if I was going to die so they could work on the other guys first. I don't know if that's true or not, but it would be common sense. They may have thought, let's get the guys we know we can help and not waste time on this guy. When they did get me, three surgeons worked for 3½ hours the first time.

Two days later, when I was coming to, I was afraid to open my eyes. I asked myself, "Am I in heaven? Am I in hell? What is this?" Before I opened my eyes, I said, "God, let it be a dream. Let it all be one nightmare. Just let it be a dream, dear God. Just let it be a dream." Then I opened my eyes and saw the white ceiling.

The gal, a Red Cross worker that was sitting by me, jumped up, and a tear streamed down her face as she said, "Welcome back, soldier."

I was afraid to look down at first, then I realized it wasn't a nightmare. My right arm was gone. "Oh, Jesus," I cried, "it really happened." It all began coming back to me.

They had a sheet stretched out from my waist down. "Have I still got my right leg, miss," I asked.

"Yes, but it's pretty serious. They might have to take it off," was her reply.

Tears started running down my face. I'm all finished as a man, I thought. Then I said to myself, "Why should I feel sorry for myself. Everyone of those guys on that hill that got killed ought to get up out of the grave and kick me," and I no longer felt sorry for myself. I thanked God right there.

I didn't understand it. Why am I alive and all those other guys are dead? I'd seen pictures of their wives and kids that they had shown me. I'd gotten to know them, gotten to know their families. I was going to go see them in the States. I felt a part of them. But I wondered, why are they dead, and I'm alive?

They brought in a television crew. They wheeled me into the other room and asked if I would talk on television. I said, "Yeah, bring them on. I'm going to tell them something." I told them what happened over there. I told them about the people that wouldn't get behind the war. And about all the guys in the rear, and how they sent us up this stupid hill—outnumbered by twenty to one. I told them everything that happened. That television tape never got out of Vietnam. It was totally censored. Somebody told me later that they'd heard me on the radio, and one of the reporters had recorded part of it and snuck it out of the country.

I was in intensive care about two weeks in the Vietnam hospital. When I was strong enough to move, they took me to Japan. It was too dangerous to move me straight to the States.

The second day in the hospital I was determined that I would write my folks a letter. It took some doing, but I made it. I was going to show everyone I was tough and could make it with one hand. There were moments I began to

Nov. 26

Dear mom and dad. how are you I am doing allrite my writeing is pretty bad because I half to write with my left hand. They change my bindages and wash my wounds 3 times a day it's a pretty painfl process The food here is great. and so is the service. they will probably start opperating on my leg in about 3 or 4 days. and than my sholder. they have my right arm in traction they are trying to strech the skin over the bone. Don't worry about me I will be good as new, it will just take a little time.

Take care God bless

Love John

P.S.
Tell everybody I'm thinking about them.

break down, but would force myself to act "macho." I really didn't realize how close I was many times to death. *God has spared me and that's that*, I thought.

I knew I was going to die on the flight to Japan. Every part of my body pulsated with pain. I was one of many arriving at the hospital. It seemed there were thousands of us arriving all at once.

As I was lying there waiting for I don't know what, I noticed a doctor approaching me. "How are you doing, soldier?" he asked.

"Give me a shot, Doc; please give me a shot," I begged.

"Let's have a look at your arm," he said as he began pulling off the bandages covering the "stump."

I screamed, "You . . . mother. I'll kill you, you S.O.B." I cursed him at the top of my lungs because it hurt so bad. I continued to scream, "God, it hurts. Oh, God, it hurts!" I lay there and cried.

For about six weeks they scrubbed me three times a day. They would literally run the cloth right through the biggest part of my right leg, wiping out the gangrene, the dead flesh. I had a bullet go through my right foot. They would take gauze and run it right through my foot. They would brush and scrape my back, getting all the dead flesh off of it. My chest was burned so they would have to keep cleaning it. After a while it got to where I could take that. It hurt, but I could take it. The last thing they'd do would be my arm. The bone was protruding almost an inch and a half past the flesh. These doctors and nurses were saints. I couldn't have done what they did. They were trying to keep me alive, but oh, how I hated them because of the pain I was suffering.

They were trying to save my elbow so they didn't clip off the bone. They glued a stump sock on my arm. The end of the sock was attached to a traction rope, in the hopes my upper arm skin would stretch enough to cover the end of the stump. They were afraid they couldn't save it because it was so infected with gangrene. As a result, they cleaned my stump three times a day, pulling back the sock and loosing the traction weights. I'd scream like a woman. I had never heard a man scream like that, but I'd scream and sometimes I'd pass out. They'd be picking around with their tweezers just to find out which nerves were alive and which nerves were dead. They took surgical knives and cut away the dead flesh. It would take several of them to hold me while they did it. This continued for six weeks, until finally they would only clean it once a day.

I got paranoid. They never gave me any shots until they were finished because they said, "With what we're doing to you, your system would just burn up the drugs right away, and they wouldn't help. If we give you enough to knock you out, we wouldn't know which nerves are good and which are bad."

I wanted to kill them. I would have, but I

couldn't because they were holding me down. I knew they were trying to help me, but that didn't stop the pain. An hour before my scrub I started shaking. I began borrowing dope off the guys who weren't going through the intense pain. I know a lot of them did, but at this time most of them weren't having it that bad. They wouldn't scream like a woman. No one seemed to scream like I did. The guys would feel sorry for me. Some of them would save up their pills by telling the nurse that they were having pain when they weren't, and they'd give me a whole handful. It still didn't do any good. Strange how one can endure pain when you have to.

It wasn't long until days became weeks. One morning I was really feeling good when the doctor came in. I sat on the bed and he said, "Steer, tomorrow we are going to start the surgery. We're going to try and put you back together. There will be skin grafts after skin grafts. We want to get your arm ready for prosthesis (artificial arm). Your infection is nearly gone, and we want to get your leg straightened out."

"Okay, Doc, I am ready. Get to it," I answered. If I would have known what torment I would go through I think I would have ended my life, but I was glad they were finally going to start putting me together.

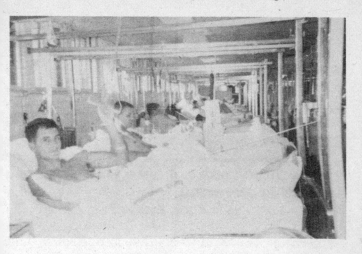

THE BROOKLYN CENTER POST
BROOKLYN CENTER, MINNESOTA, THURSDAY, DECEMBER 28, 1967

He Answered the Call

LIKE HUNDREDS of other servicemen from this area, John L. Steer of 5801 Bryant ave. N., didn't complain when he entered the service. Today, he's confined to a field hospital in Vietnam with most of his right arm missing. Steer was hit by enemy fire on hill 875 at Dak To on Nov. 21. He was on the operating table three and one-half hours as three surgeons removed bullets from his right leg and shoulder and shrapnel from his left thigh and chest. His right arm was amputated below the elbow. Despite all this, his parents report his spirit as "good". This week, Post newspapers are printing pictures of many area servicemen, and the editors feel John L. Steer deserves page one as a typical American young man who answered the call. As Steer and all loved ones know, there are many who will never come back. To all these young men fighting for their country: WELL DONE!

9
BACK TO THE STATES

I was so thankful to be alive in one sense, and yet in another, sorry and guilty. I was alive and all those good guys were dead. I was no good, and I was alive. I was starting to get all mixed up in my head. Insane thoughts would come and go. Strange things started happening to me at night.

Some army truck drivers were telling war stories while visiting a friend there at the hospital. I had had it, and I didn't want to hear one more war story or anything about the war. I simply couldn't handle it. I went berserk, broke the ropes on my traction for the arms and legs, and went in for the kill. To me the room became a battleground, and I was going to kill everyone in the room. I dragged a warrant officer out of bed that had just had surgery, and because of that, had to have surgery again. I also hit a real nice nurse and a doctor. I guess I battered up several people, but I didn't remember any of it.

They finally held me down and gave me a shot

that knocked me out. They put me in bed and began bandaging up all my wounds because I'd busted everything open. Wayne Lombardo told me that five minutes later I was back on top of this truck driver trying to kill him. They gave me another shot, which I guess could have killed me, but they had to do something to keep me from killing myself and everybody in the room.

The darkness that surrounded me at night was almost unbearable. I thought I was living in hell. I couldn't find God anywhere. I'd wake up in the middle of the night screaming, thinking I was back in Vietnam going through the June 22 battle over and over. When I didn't go through that one, I'd make up one of my own in my mind. I'd kill the same gook over and over and over. I'd never seen that gook, but he'd be in my dreams every night. I knew I was slipping in my mind and didn't know what to do. Even in this condition I was still a paratrooper and a big shot.

I had my knife hid under my pillow, and most days I still thought I was in Vietnam. In my mind everybody was out to get me. Wayne was the same way, and I was so glad that he was there with me because I could talk to him. He had lost his shoulder.

I had to take a knife away from him one day because he said to one of the orthopedic surgeons that cut on him so much, "I'm going to cut on you a while." He cornered the doctor and was going to kill him. I talked him into giving the knife to me. He wouldn't give it to anybody else. He would have killed me also, but I was his friend.

I got where I could get out of bed. I'd put lead weights on the end of my stump, my heel, and I'd get on crutches and hobble around. I started then to sneak out at night and go into town, trying to find a prostitute. I never found one, but I'd get drunk. How pitiful I must have looked, wandering the streets of Tokyo.

The lights were flashing like a million flash cubes going off and kept me from thinking. The booze helped me forget. I was an eighteen-year-old armless and near-legless freak.

I paid a sergeant in the hospital to keep my water jug full of whiskey. I was getting demerol every four hours. I would cry like a baby so they'd bring me more of it—that and the whiskey were my peace. I was hooked and a junky on prescribed medicine.

I was sneaking off base, but they all humored me. The nurses knew, of course. Everybody knew it. They'd threaten me at times, but I'd fire back, "There's nothing you can do."

There is a point in a person's life when there isn't anything that can scare you. I'd been to hell and back, and here they were threatening me with jail. I simply went ahead and did what I wanted.

One night the Colonel came in and said, "Steer?"

"Yes, sir," I replied.

"When you sneak out of here tonight, I want you to take the kid next to you along. He's really down in the dumps." I didn't know that the Colonel knew that I was sneaking out. I didn't think the nurses would squeal on me.

I took the kid who had one leg off to the train station. We got on a train going to a little village near Tokyo to get drunk. I didn't know where we were going. I didn't have any Japanese money, but man, I could always make a way. I couldn't speak Japanese, but we made it. I had whiskey in one pocket and Maalox in the other (I had a bleeding ulcer). We both got drunk and cried and cried over our mutual troubles. The next day neither of us remembered how we got back to the hospital.

The surgery continued, and somehow I managed to endure the trauma day by day. Fear dominated my every waking hour, along with questions such as: What can I do with only one arm? Does anyone care? Does anyone love me? How long before I see my folks? Will Dad be proud of me? How I longed to be home in the good old U.S.A.

I was constantly begging the doctors, "When will I be well enough to go to the States?" The answer was always the same: "When we think you can stand the trip home."

My drinking was becoming a serious problem, and I knew it! My quiet bewilderment about still being alive when my buddies were dead was difficult to cope with, and often I didn't. The doctors, I believe, were more concerned about my mental health than my physical status.

I tried so hard to act normal, and it paid off.

Soon I was given a date when I would be transferred to the Great Lakes Naval Hospital in Illinois. Talk about excited! I was ready and yet somewhat afraid.

As I was taken aboard the plane on the litter, I couldn't help shedding a few tears. Why was I going home and so many of my buddies would never get home unless it was in a box? My mind really was running away with itself, and I was not able to stop it. Seemingly I was three or four personalities—in a disfigured body at that.

I was excited about returning home and wanted to see my folks. I really missed them and needed them in a special way at this time.

Even though I had been at death's door and had seen the hand of God on my life, I was still rebellious and full of hate. I was constantly in and out of trouble.

Soon after I arrived at the hospital my folks came from Minneapolis to see me. I hadn't seen them for about a year and could hardly stand the suspense of waiting. What would it be like to see them? Would they be proud of me and think I had matured? My whole being was wanting some love, but when they got there Dad was about half tight. I'm sure it was the only way he could face me. I recalled one of the last things he had said to me, "John, Vietnam won't be any worse than what I've seen."

The first thing Dad said as he put out his hand was "How many S.O.B.'s did you kill?" I shook his hand instead of letting my hair down and telling them that I was lonely. I wanted some love. You know—hugs and kisses—but instead, I put on the tough guy image, which was what I felt they expected. Our conversation was bland, and about 99% of the blame was mine. I was too proud to admit to myself, or them, that I was in need.

I was at Great Lakes a couple of months. My routine was surgery after surgery. I had a few weeks out of the hospital before I was sent to Fitzsimons Hospital in Denver.

The folks were anxious for me to come home. Dad, God bless him, fixed me a special room in the basement. He went to a lot of trouble once again to show me how much he cared, but I just couldn't let him know how grateful I really was. I was so hard that I couldn't show love or hardly even say "Thanks." Most of my friends were dead, and I couldn't bring myself to grips about anything. So I lost an arm, I thought—the rest are dead. Then it was good-bye again and off to the hospital in Denver.

When I was in Nam I used to pray, "Don't let me get hit in the face or my right arm." I was pretty proud of my right arm. I had a good right upper cut, but that's what I lost. Afterwards I felt that I was alive and all those guys were dead—so I'd better not complain. I didn't worry about what I was going to do without my right arm. There again, they didn't allow me to worry. Right away they started telling me, "Man, you're going to get a pension. It will be more money than you could ever make working, and we're going to give you an arm that is just great."

What I was really thinking about was: How am I going to hug a woman or how am I going to punch somebody in the nose? Besides, how was I going to get a woman? Who is going to be interested in this one-arm mutilated guy?

The purpose of going to Fitzsimons was to be fitted for a prosthesis (hook), and be taught how to use it. Some of the guys had been there for two years, and in my case it took quite a while also because I still had sores on my stump. Some of the guys had to be operated on again and again just to make the prosthesis fit and get a flap of protection over the bone. I had more surgery like that, too.

The guys that I was with were all crippled, and we were assigned to run the automatic elevator. I was supposed to keep the men scheduled and there. I was always rebellious, having a lot of trouble with the officers, etc. I told the guys that I didn't care if they showed for duty or not. I was a sergeant over a platoon of men that was supposed to run the automatic elevators—some detail! I really felt important!

The elevators had always been automatic, but they had us cripples, some of them with no legs, some with no arms, some with wire braces, and some with every other kind of weird contraption and condition you can imagine—they wanted us to stay in these automatic elevators like a bunch of freaks and push the buttons for people. They must have had some reason or other for it, but we didn't know what it was. I was working in a bar off base (actually AWOL), instead of running the elevators.

There was a competition among the men to try to do good with their artificial limbs. We'd go to the park with a case of beer and sit around like a bunch of monstrosities. I'd throw my artificial arm off that I was using temporarily, and pull on another guy's artificial leg and pull it off. The people would drive by in cars and probably think we were crazy, and we were.

One day one of the guys at the park wanted to prove he could drive with wooden legs. The car he was going to drive was somebody else's souped-up one. Once a car is properly equipped it isn't hard to drive with wooden legs. Because you don't have any feeling in an artificial leg they have adaptive equipment on the steering wheel so you can control it with your hands. He got in the car, stepped on the gas and lost control of the car, and ran over a little kid. He went crazy and was put in a mental institution right after it happened. He ended up committing suicide.

There was also this constant competition to try and prove that you could do anything with your artificial limbs that you always could do with real limbs.

At first they put padding on my stump and made a mold form that would fit in a universal arm. I got so I could use it fairly well. Then came the day I finally got my own arm fitted just for me. I was very excited about it, and I'd practice using it for hours every day. You were supposed to carry like four bands—which was quite a bit of strength. I would carry twenty-six, which was just a spirit in me trying to prove that I could do better than anybody else. Nobody had ever carried that kind of strength—at the end of my hook were rubber bands until it looked like a golf ball or bigger. These were used to close the hooks and clamp very tight.

A young lady lieutenant at the rehab used to get so mad at me for carrying so much strength and doing all the things I could do. "Steer," she hollered at me one day, "you wear that arm more like a medal than something you're ashamed of." Her problem was that she was ashamed of it, and I wasn't.

I told her, "Well, honey, it is like a medal to me because all those guys that are dead would get up and kick my butt if they'd see me feeling sorry for myself."

To learn to use a hook just takes a half hour, or hour, but then to become proficient with it, you have to use it and do things with it over and over. I taught people how to shuffle cards. They'd never known how to shuffle cards with a hook before, but I figured out how to do it. I taught them how to light a cigarette lighter. They'd never seen anybody light a cigarette lighter with it before. I learned to do many things. I raced motorcycles with it later, but I learned to do things that other people couldn't do with it continually.

I was called to the Colonel's office one day. He

was head of Fitzsimons Hospital. He said, "Steer, we're having some complaints on you, that you're wearing too much strength on your hook. There's no reason for that. You are going to harm your other muscles."

"Yes, sir, there are reasons," I answered.

"What are your reasons?"

I went into the corner of his office, very rebellious, but deliberately, to where he had this big, high, green wastebasket. It was about half full of paper. I reached down and picked it up (it was a metal can) with my hook. I held it out and said, "There isn't anybody else in the rehab center that can do this because they don't have the strength to pick it up."

"But you'll crush things if you've got too much strength," he replied.

I then went over to the ash tray on his desk. I picked up an ash off of his cigarette and didn't break it—and I handed it to him. He was dumbfounded and beside himself when I left.

I'd go off base when I wanted to. I worked in a bar at night, leaving without a pass. I did what I wanted to. I'd even go out of there in my pajamas many times. I frequently said a Russian Battalion could go through the gate and they'd salute them.

I was forever trying to prove to everybody what I could do with my hook. I got a job at one bar. Here I was a sergeant in the army, looking for a job, but I was only nineteen years old. I hung out at this one place called the End Zone. Jim McMillian was the owner. He was one of the

Bronco's. I hung out there and asked him for a job. Because of my hook, he wouldn't hire me.

"John, we really don't need anybody right now," was always the reply.

"Look, I need some money. I really need some money. Can't you give me some kind of a job?"

"Well, I suppose if you want to, you could pull weeds around the building," he answered.

I went outside and pulled weeds on my hands and knees. For about three days I pulled the weeds, and I pulled them the best I could. I was still sore all over. I wasn't even supposed to be walking much on my leg, but I finally got all the weeds pulled. After a while they hired me as a night man at the door to check the I.D. cards. I checked I.D. cards to make sure the persons coming in were twenty-one—and I was just nineteen!

I liked the fact that my hook impressed people, but I didn't like people staring at me either unless I wanted them to. If I'd go in a place and people would stare at me, I'd get up and walk to their table and ask what was the matter with them, and try to get them to fight.

I got a pass for a couple of weeks to go home. I took a girl with me. They'd given me a whole big box of bandages for the sores on my legs; they were draining at the bottom of the scars. They'd sewn it up, but there would be a sore someplace where it would drain. The skin grafts, too, were still kind of messy.

Soon after we were home, I got tired of the girl so I threw a couple of hundred bucks on the bed and told her to get a plane and get out of my life. She didn't do it. She stayed with my folks while I dated other girls and lived with them. When I came back she was still there, so I took her back to the base. I put her out of the car at one point and told her to walk. I was heartless.

I never went without my arm. I didn't go across the street without it. I'd go to bed without it, but that was it.

I returned then to the hospital and went before the board where I was evaluated 100% disabled. Then I was shipped home with a bunch of bandages because I still had some little sores on my stump, and my other wounds were also still draining.

John L. Steer, 5801 Bryant ave. N., has been awarded the Silver Star for gallantry in action in Vietnam.

He is a specialist four E4 with the United States Army 2nd battalion, 503d Infantry, 173d Airborne Brigade.

On Nov. 19, Steer's platoon was securing the landing zone for the purpose of extracting Company A's sister elements when word was received that a large North Vietnamese force was approaching from the rear.

JOHN STEER

Steer immediately moved to the rear and assumed the most favorable defensive position to place heavy fire on the enemy.

As company A began regrouping to fight its way back, Steer, without order, remained in his highly exposed position despite the withering volume of automatic weapons, grenade and mortar fire with only a few men to aid him in holding off the large enemy force until the rear was secure.

When he was sure the rear was safe, he immediately moved to the front which was the scene of vicious fighting. It was there that he was seriously wounded.

Although wounded, Steer continued to move from position to position, refusing medical aid and assisting in repulsing the enemy's counter-attack.

He moved forward of the perimeter to drag a wounded comrade to safety, completely ignoring the enemy's fire and the seriousness of his own wound.

His display of courage, initiative and complete disregard for his personal safety was in the highest traditions of the military service and reflect great credit upon himself, his unit and the United States Army according to George S. Blanchard, Brigadier General.

Steer, who was hit by enemy fire on Hill 875 at Dak To, was on the operating table for three - and-a-half hours as three surgeons removed bullets from his right leg and shoulder and shrapnel from his thigh and chest.

His right arm was amputated below the elbow. He was featured in a picture taken at the hospital in a December front page of The Brooklyn Center Post.

Steer is in Fitzsimons Army hospital in Denver, but was home for two weeks in April. He is waiting to be discharged.

Steer has also received the Purple Heart, two Purple Hearts with clusters, the Bronze Star and the Army accommodation medal.

On July 6 Steer will be married to Donna Rick of Breckenridge.

10
DONNA

I met Donna at a nightclub called "The Store." Donna was a quiet, not-the-talkative type; always afraid of doing dangerous and exciting things. She wouldn't even ride horses because her folks said she might fall off and break an arm. Motorcycles were also out because she might fall off and get hurt.

Everything I did was danger and excitement. But wait a minute, she could tell it better than I.

My girl friend and I had gone to "The Store" on a dare. The fellow that was with John came up to us and started talking. He told me he had a friend that would join us. "He's been in Vietnam, lost his arm, and he's from Minnesota," he said.

When he said, "Minnesota," I thought I'd like to meet him—that's where I was from. I was real excited about meeting him. When his friend said, "one arm," I thought, This poor boy's been in Vietnam and lost an arm—inside he really wants pity. However, when I met him I could see that he didn't want any pity. When he started talking it was like we had always known each other.

His having one arm didn't bother me then, and never has in the passing years, because the night I met him he could do anything with his hook—anything anybody else could do. He was lighting cigarettes, flicking the lighters, opening doors, etc., and did that ever impress me!

After a whirlwind romance, John was discharged from the hospital and we went to Minnesota to get married. We had a big church wedding with all the trimmings. John wasn't getting his VA pension yet so we had almost no money. I went to work. John would go to get a job and people wouldn't hire him because of his one arm.

Our days and weeks ahead consisted of one party after another—dancing, drinking, and night clubs. The first year we were married John was in the hospital almost nine months. I loved him and had him up on this pedestal—like he was God and couldn't do anything wrong.

He would wake up in the night screaming and thrashing all over the bed. One night I woke up and he was dreaming he was in Vietnam and just about killed me. A lot of times he'd try to put his stump through the wall. As soon as I heard him begin to have a nightmare I would stand in the doorway and yell at him until I finally got him awakened. If I would try to shake him, he'd reach out and was ready to kill me, so I knew better than to do that, or stand close to wake him up.

I also learned never to go behind him and grab him because he'd turn around swinging. It was all from Vietnam, and I realized that, so I wasn't afraid of him. I wasn't afraid for my life.

John simply couldn't calm down. He had to be doing something every waking moment. Even when I was pregnant he'd have the motorcycle out front and tell me, "Get on. We're going for a ride." We would then tear down the highway at almost a hundred miles an hour.

Everything was fine up until we had our first baby girl, Monique. I then determined that I wasn't going to take her to all the bars, nightclubs, and everything else. I wasn't going to leave her with the babysitter either.

When I had the baby John didn't even come to the hospital during the delivery. I was hurt that he wasn't there, but I couldn't do anything about it. A lot of times I just kept all the hurt inside of me. I didn't have anybody to talk to. I had a sister living in Denver, but I couldn't confide in her because if I did, she'd call my folks in Minnesota and tell them all the problems. I didn't want my folks to know about the problems we were having.

We didn't have any close friends. We had all his drinking buddies, but I couldn't even talk to John. If he'd go out and get drunk I wouldn't talk to him for maybe three days. I couldn't say

one word without him going into a rage. It
became worse and worse.

One time he had been out drinking for a couple
of days and when he came home my folks were
visiting. I asked John, "May I go home with my
folks?"

He got so mad that he put his stump through
the window, and I had to take him to the army
hospital so he could have his stump sewed up. I
told everybody how he walked into the window.
I began lying and making excuses for him.

Sometimes I couldn't take any more and then
I would say something. One time he wrecked the
coffee table, and another time he put his fist
through the door. I got to the point where I was
so tired of him wrecking the furniture that I
almost wanted him to hit me, but he never did.

After the baby was born we moved back to the
Denver area so we could be near the hospital. He
started going to what was called a day hospital
in Denver to see a psychiatrist. They really
wanted to admit him full-time, but he wouldn't
stand for that. If he didn't feel like going, he
didn't go. If he felt like going, he would go but
usually he spent all day in the bar.

I'd leave for work and he'd still be in bed, but
then he'd hit the bars and play pool all day. He
usually picked me up from work, and we'd go
out to eat supper and then hit the bars or
nightclubs until 2:00 A.M. Then I'd go to bed
and get up and go to work.

After he had a few too many drinks under his
belt, he would begin to cry. Between sobs he'd

say, "Why am I alive and the friends of mine from Vietnam all dead? I wish I were dead." He'd cry like that, and I couldn't understand why. I couldn't understand how someone could say "I wish I were dead." Why wasn't he happy? I was happy, or at least was most of the time. I really loved him, and I guess that was stronger than all the negative things. Most of the problem was mental anguish.

One night during work, they brought him home, and he was shaking and couldn't stop. Then his head began pounding and he began screaming. This also affected his sight, so they put him in a padded cell and kept him there for ten days.

There were times that John would be sweet and normal, but not very often.

One time I thought I would get even with John for the way he treated me. He had a friend that he met in the hospital. His friend's wife came over one Saturday afternoon, and it was raining so I couldn't wash clothes. I told John I needed some Pampers for Monique. She offered to drive me to town to get them.

I said, "Okay," and we took off. She suggested that we stop and have a drink. John had just been out drinking and had gotten home that morning. I was really mad at him. I said to my friend, "Okay, that would be fine." We sat down and started talking and drinking. We stayed there for about four or five hours. Then she said, "Why don't we drive into Denver and go dancing?"

"Okay, that sounds real good and should be fun." I didn't want to do it. I was afraid, but I wanted some way to get even and thought this would be a good way. I'd been sitting home night after night wondering where he was, and if he were dead or alive. *Now you can just sit and worry about me!* I thought, and so we took off and went to Denver dancing.

I didn't get home until 1:00 A.M. When we walked in the door he was mad. "Where have you been?" He had called the State Patrol and had them looking for us. Instead of taking it out on me he got real nasty with my friend. He never did bawl me out at the time, but boy, he was ready to kill her. He almost punched her right there and then.

She had a mouth anyway and talked right back to him. Finally, she had to get out of the house or he'd have thrown her out. She got out fast. I told her she had better leave because I knew that he'd really do something like that. So she left and then he started bawling me out. He got so mad, instead of hitting me, he put his fist through the coffee table.

Five years we lived in that constant turmoil. I was beginning to wonder if it would ever end, but one day it suddenly ended.

John's mother and father

**Sarah, John, Donna, David
John Jr., Monique**

11
THE WAY OUT

"God, why am I alive? Why are my buddies dead and I'm alive?" I asked myself that question over and over every day. I was crazy and lived in constant fear. I would examine every person I met and tried to figure out how to kill them. I would imagine that they had a gun in their pocket or a grenade, or knife, or machine gun in the trunk of their car. It was so real to me. Everybody I'd see I thought was going to kill me. Especially if I couldn't see them, if I heard a noise or something like that.

I was going to the head shrinkers, and was repulsed by them. I had two lady head shrinkers. They thought to make you feel at home they had to talk like pigs. They talked worse than most guys in Vietnam. I guess they were trying to make me loosen up and feel at home, but it just appalled me. Here were nice-looking young ladies that talked like pigs, and I didn't know what they were trying to get out of me.

The migraine headaches had started by now. They were terrible, terrible headaches. That's when they started giving me dope. They started me on mellaril. Nothing seemed to help me. I wondered why I was alive. I was always mad because I was alive.

I was going to the psychiatrist regularly. I went to a big hospital where they had a bunch of crazies in there, and we'd all sit around and talk about our problems. I can't see where it helped much.

My poor wife didn't know what I was getting into next. I'd bring over the Hell's Angels to the apartment and ride my motorcycle through the house. I'd go to the day hospital, and during the whole time I was taking more and more mellaril. Soon they switched me to valium—which was stronger. The nightmares, the migraine headaches—after a while they got to hospitalizing me a couple of times because it got to where I was about to go blind with pain. I'd be screaming, following the psychiatrist through the hospital like a whipped pup, begging for dope to take the pain away from my head. The only way they could do that was to put me on the crazy floor in a padded room and give me a shot of dope every four hours. I was in there one time for ten days. I didn't know when I came in, and I just barely remember coming out. My dad came to see me. Donna had come to see me several times. It must have killed them that I didn't even know they came.

I was still wanting to prove myself, wanting

to work. So I joined the VFW and ended up managing the bar at the VFW. By now my army pension started coming. I still felt bad that Donna was working and I wasn't. I'd sit around the house afraid. The day hospital was good in one sense because it got me out of the house.

When I would go into a bar, I would start trouble, trying to attack this fear and making up things in my mind like: *This guy doesn't like me. I'm going to get him.* I was always looking for something; forever searching, but I didn't know for what.

We started going to a psychic church where they read your mind and stuff. I thought: *That's kind of neat,* but I soon saw that it was phony. There were some familiar spirits there too, and it was all a bunch of garbage.

I wanted to be a cop, so I went to take the test at the Police Department. They let me go through all the tests. I passed everything until I came to the physical. They wouldn't let me take it and told me I couldn't pass that because I wouldn't be able to apprehend a criminal.

I grabbed the doctor by his tie with my hook. He quickly said, "I'm sorry, man. We've got a policy, and with your hook, you can't be a policeman." But he had let me take all the exams and tests and everything else first before he told me that. I guess he was hoping that I would flunk out before I got to the physical. I was upset about that and started thinking: *I'm not a man. My wife is working, and I'm not working.*

I then applied at the Post Office. I heard that veterans had preference. I took all their tests, and they said, "Yes, you passed it. We'll get you a desk job."

I said, "I don't want a desk job. I want a route. I want to be on the street." I was still trying to prove myself. My legs were still hurting, but I didn't consider them. I had to prove to myself that I could do anything. I got a route after I fought it to the top. After I got the job, I couldn't handle it. It wasn't my hook that gave me the trouble, it was my leg that couldn't handle it, so I quit—defeated again!

After two or three months, I started working for a junk yard, cutting up cars—running with this guy, drinking all the time and smoking dope. Pretty soon I was back seeing the head shrinkers in Denver. They set me up again on a day hospital program. They started me out on 30 mg. of valium a day and then increased it to 40 mg. Then it increased to where it said on the bottle that I was to "take this and eat at will."

I had hyperventilation, migraine headaches, and pain in my arms, my legs, and my back—suffering beyond belief. I guess most of it was in my gut from where I was remembering Vietnam every night. It was just terrible.

I cheated on my wife, and I felt terrible about that. That almost killed me. I had to tell her. My psychiatrist told me to tell her. Again, it was selfish to get the guilt off me, and put it on her. It pretty near killed her.

We weren't long in Denver when I made

friends with some people in organized crime. I constantly felt I had to prove myself. The same old spirit kept rising up. One of my best friends was an abortionist. I thought that was horrible. I hated what he did. I didn't know about it for a long time, but he was in the Mafia. He was a big shot with them. He was a medical doctor that had lost his license. It wasn't just abortions, but he did whatever came—whatever they needed.

When I met him, I thought I was with big time now. "John," he said, "people are going to have dope anyway, so we can supply it. We're just business men," and he convinced me. He saw how rebellious I was, how I'd get in trouble, fights and stuff, and one day he asked, "Steer, could you kill somebody?"

"Yeah, I could kill somebody if there were a reason. I've killed lots of people. If there's a reason, sure."

"Now what if somebody was coming against our organization. We're just trying to be decent people and sell dope and stuff. What about that?"

"For a price I could kill . . . sure."

"Steer," he said, "I have some important men I want you to meet. With me you are going to go places. You can make a lot of money. You can do good, but when we go in there you've got a big mouth—just keep it shut. I'll do all the talking. You just shut up."

I did. I met three or four guys. Apparently they were talking about a contract.

A few days later I found some drunks that I

liked better than him so we moved away. That's how I was—sporadic. We'd drive around, drunk, in my Fiat, on the ice when there was two inches of ice on the lake. I can see God's hand on it now, how He used those drunks to get me out of organized crime before I got really involved.

I went from one job to another, but nothing satisfied me. I was dragging Donna around all over the country. We finally bought a house near Longmont, fixed it up and raised some hogs and 200 rabbits. We'd been married two years now. Donna got pregnant. I didn't even show up when she had the baby—I was drunk. I worked hard all the time. I'd bring people to the house, and I'd call her filthy names and treat her like dirt. I don't know why, because I loved her, but I treated her like dirt.

By this time I wanted to quit drinking, but I couldn't. Back to the shrinks. Every once in a while I'd go bonkers, or just start shaking and couldn't control myself. Donna would take me to the hospital, and they'd shoot me full of dope.

My aunt Elaine wrote me a letter about Arkansas and told how beautiful it was. I'd been through there as a kid so I told Donna, "Let's go to Arkansas." It was just like that—here we've just settled in our house and had five acres when I said, "Let's sell this and go to Arkansas."

She said, "We don't know anybody in Arkansas."

"Well, I have an uncle there. Let's go."

We found a forty-acre farm and bought it. Within three or four months we moved.

While in Arkansas, again I had to prove myself. I got in a fight with a big guy in town as soon as I moved. We moved to a dry county, and I tried to get the county wet. I'd never heard of any such thing as "dry." I'd have never bought the place if I'd known I had to drive forty miles to get a drink, but I did. I couldn't get anybody to go with me to get the booze, so I started bootlegging.

I was always looking for something. Just to kind of narrow it on down, this is five years now from the time that I got out of the service. It was five years of the same lies—just different places, just living like a pig. I stayed drunk all the time.

A telephone lineman was working on the telephone pole at the farm and asked me, "Are you a Christian?"

"Yeah, sure. God brought me through Vietnam. I'll always remember God," I answered.

A seed was planted.

The doctors had told me that I had black spots on my lungs. I was smoking four packs of cigarettes a day. Then there was all the booze I was drinking. I was eating the valium like candy. By this time I'd made it up with the doctor where Donna could take me in and they'd give me a whole bag of syringes full of demerol. I'd go home and shoot it in my leg. My mind was going. Most of the time I couldn't tell you what day it was, and I didn't care. I drove a hundred miles an hour almost every place I went. I wrecked three trucks one year.

I was so afraid of people finding out that I didn't know anything. When I'd come in at night I'd trained Donna to write down whatever I said. I might mention about that I was supposed to go fishing the next day or do something, and the next morning when I woke up I knew that I wouldn't remember, but with her writing it down I'd learned to function fairly well as an alcoholic where people didn't know that I didn't remember anything the next day.

I laid awake one whole night and cried out to God saying, "God, I want to kill myself. My daughter has an incurable illness. I've made my wife's life miserable. I'm miserable. If this is all there is to life, I want to die. But I'm still afraid if I did, I'd go to hell." I was always thinking that maybe I could con God and slip into eternity in a car accident or something, but I knew it wouldn't work that way.

I got up the next morning and didn't smoke or drink. I kept taking the valium because I told myself that was medicine. I cursed my wife. Oh, how I cursed my wife. I begged her to leave because I was in withdrawals. I was having these withdrawals and I didn't want her to see them, plus she was so good. That made me feel so rotten. She was just always so good.

Monique, our daughter, was an epileptic. There she was a drug addict at two years old taking double the maximum doses of phenobarbitol. She couldn't even walk, except from furniture to furniture because of the effect that it had on her. I knew that all this was because of me.

I started looking for God so—we began going to the Baptist church. I took Donna, but all that happened was that I got religion and self-righteous. All my friends left me. Now I was really mad because my drinking buddies wouldn't come out to the house. I'd tell my old buddies, "Bring your booze and come out to the house." I had a $700 pool table there. I had a building that I'd built for bootlegging. I had quit doing that so I said, "Just bring your booze and come out." They wouldn't do it.

At the Baptist church they said that you had to accept Jesus Christ as your Saviour. I knew God, but they said God had made a plan for our lives and it's Jesus. So I went forward to the altar and prayed, "Jesus, I accept You as my Saviour. Forgive me my sins." But, I mean nothing happened. It was just words. I got up and people patted me on the back, but I didn't believe God heard me.

I thought, *maybe I've got to get baptized*. So I was baptized. Nothing happened—or at least it didn't seem so to me. I was getting more and more frustrated at this religion because I thought, *I'm loosing so much. I don't have my dope, and I'm still having withdrawals. I want to do right. I really want to do right in my heart, but I can't make it anyway—why try?*

God sent a man to me. Bill came to the house

one day and said, "Hey, I heard you're a Christian."

My attitude was, "If there was ever a Christian, that's me," I was just going along with this thing, trying to be one.

Bill shared with me about the baptism in the Holy Spirit. The first time I met him he started speaking in tongues in my living room. I'd never heard of such a thing. I said, "Man, you are crazy!" He's showing me these things in the Word. When I had enough I'd send him away.

One Sunday the pastor at this little Baptist church said, "We believe this from cover to cover," and was holding up the Holy Bible. Something hit me. If I was going to really walk this walk and find God, I was going to have to also believe His Word—all of it—whether I agreed with it or not—I had to believe it.

I said to Donna, "I'm going to read the Bible and believe it all, although I don't understand it."

When Bill showed me these things about the baptism of the Holy Spirit, here I am saying, "That's crazy," but the Spirit was talking to me: "You said you were going to believe it all." Bill left, but he kept coming back, planting seeds.

I'm still miserable. I'm religious, and I'm miserable. I've lost my friends. I'm mad at God because I've lost my friends. I'm still having the nightmares. I'm still sitting up until the last television show goes off the air—afraid to go to bed because when I went to sleep I knew I was going to have a bad dream.

Bill keeps coming back. "I want to see John," he'd say.

I'd tell my wife, "Tell him I'm sick." He didn't care. He was going to pray for me, so he'd push his way into the house and pray for me. Finally I got to liking him a little. I went down to his house a couple of times to talk with him. Bill was just a few years older than me.

Bill then started coming to the house every day, and he was driving me nuts. He'd follow around while I was trying to get away from him showing me Scriptures. He wouldn't let me go. "John," he asked, "are you reading the Word?"

"Well, when I read my eyes water up, and I can't see anything." I had better than 20-20 vision because I went to the doctor and had my eyes checked, but every time I picked up a Bible my eyes would water and get red to where I couldn't see. I could read anything else and never had any eye problems, just with the Bible.

Instead of giving up on me, Bill brings me the whole Bible on records, and brought his record player too. I put it out in my pool hall, my building outside that I'd had for bootlegging before I quit. I would shoot pool all night and listen to the Bible.

The first month I venture to say I went through the whole Bible twice, seventy-six hours of it. God would quicken something to me, always a different Scripture. I was really wrestling with the power of the Word.

Bill kept asking me if I wanted the baptism of the Holy Spirit. I said, "No, I don't. It's crazy."

Bill showed me he loved me, and it didn't matter what or who I was. All the time the Word is building faith in me while I'm shooting pool all night until I'd get so tired I'd finally collapse in bed. Eventually it worked on me until I said, "I'm going to try this baptism thing. I am going to surrender everything to God." I had a quarter mile driveway and could see people coming and I didn't want anybody to see me praying so I locked the doors. I seemed to pray for hours.

I'm still going to the Baptist church. I was leading the choir and doing other things, but it was a facade. It was a phony thing. They said they knew they were saved, but I didn't know I was saved. I wasn't, but I thought they were lying. If they weren't lying I wanted to find out what they had. I know now the key was that I'd never repented.

Two nights in a row I got down on my knees, shut the lights off, locked the door, pulled the curtains in my little building and prayed, "God, if there is something in this baptism of the Holy Spirit, give it to me." Nothing happened, and felt like a thousand people were laughing at me. I felt terrible. I'd smash the balls around the table. I'd be frustrated, but the Word is still going. These seventy-eight records are still always going, the Word, the Word.

I did the same thing the next night, and I got up and smashed the balls again. I was ready to chuck the whole works, the whole religious mess. It was getting ridiculous. I was making a fool of myself. I was really ready to give it up.

One night at 10 P.M. I got a phone call from Bill. He said, "John, do you believe in praying for the sick?"

Then I recalled that God delivered me from Vietnam, and the Scriptures in the Bible that I'd heard said so. I answered, "Yes, I guess so."

"Well, John, my little girl is really sick and would you come over and pray for her?"

I thought that the guy was a little dingy. Suddenly, before I knew what happened I said, "Sure, Bill, I'll come over," and hung up the phone.

I turned to Donna and said, "Honey, Bill wants me to come and pray with him for his little girl that's sick—and go through some ritual of laying on of hands or something like that. I don't know what he's going to do, but I'm going to go and make sure that he takes her to the hospital afterwards." That was my motive for going: to make sure he didn't let that little girl die.

My heart was seeking for God so I was willing to do anything. When I got to the house his little girl was laying on the couch. I felt her head, and she was burning up with fever.

"Bill, what do we do?" I asked.

"Put your hand on her."

"Where?"

"Just put your hand on her head."

"Okay, now what?"

"Ask God to please heal her," he said.

"Okay," I replied. Then I said, "God, I want You to heal her." Her head became cool under my fingertips. I felt the presence of God in the room, and I began to see myself as unclean, filthy, stinking, just no good. I repented and cried out to God on my face, crying and bawling and squalling. All this sin that I'd committed that I'd never repented of, I began now to repent. "God, forgive me of this and that." Now I knew that God was hearing me, and Jesus was my Saviour. MY SAVIOUR!

Bill then asked, "Now do you want the baptism of the Holy Spirit?"

"I guess so. If there's more, I want it."

At that remark Bill and his wife laid hands on me and began to pray. Demon spirits began to manifest themselves in me, and I didn't know what was happening. I felt I was going crazy again when they started pestering me. I started stuttering and cursing God in what sounded like Vietnamese, or at least some oriental language. Then I heard Bill pray, "Come out of him in the name of Jesus." And I'm saying to myself: *How can I come out of me in the name of Jesus. I'm going crazy again—I'm going to end up in the mental ward.*

Shortly, as they prayed for me, the room of my being seemed to be clean, swept, and garnished. I understand now what happened. I didn't then. I was sitting on the floor empty, and I believe to this day it's better to be full of demons than to be empty. When you're empty, you are nothing. I was like a little bug. Somebody could have stepped on me, and I wouldn't have cared. When I was controled by Satan I thought I was something. I came in there thinking that I had it together, and I'm tough and I can handle it. Drop me by parachute any place in the world, and I'll make it. Now I couldn't do anything. I was a little bug, and I needed something. I needed love. I needed Jesus. I needed His Holy Spirit.

They said, "Now God will fill you with the Holy Spirit."

I saw the door and wanted to run for it, but I was too afraid. They prayed—nothing happened. Then I said, "Now look you guys, I have already quit smoking, drinking, cursing and cheating on my wife. What more does God want?"

"God wants your all, John . . . your all," said Bill.

"No way. God can't have my all. Look here, God, this is where I quit."

Then Bill said something very wise: "John, God doesn't want your habits. He wants you."

They were about ready to give up on me. I went to another room by myself and got down on my knees. I was very honest with God and said, "God, I don't know who You are. How can I trust You with my life and give You everything? I don't understand it."

The Holy Spirit would remind me how He delivered me from Vietnam, how when somebody was holding a gun in my stomach and they could have just squeezed the trigger, yet He delivered me. Then the love of God surrounded me and I heard Him speak: "Trust Me, trust Me."

I prayed, "God, I'm going to trust You for a few seconds but You've got to prove to me that this is all real, that it's really You."

As soon as I yielded to Him in the Spirit— nobody was praying for me, nobody was laying hands on me—I went out like a light. My nose and my face hit the floor. God gave me such love that I'd never had in my whole life. I mean I was crying and laughing at the same time. This love seemed to run out of me—and me—I was out of me. I saw beautiful colors all around me—beautiful, beautiful colors and heard warm, lovely music. This doesn't happen to everyone—but it did to me.

The others came into the room and I said, "You won't believe where I am. It's beautiful here." It was like I was standing there. It wasn't like I was in a dream or on my face at all. "If you could be here—if you could just come and see this! It is so beautiful. There's love and Jesus is here! Thank You, Jesus."

Then I saw a black staircase in the middle of this beautiful light and music and warmth. There was a baby on the first step. Later the Lord showed me that this was me just starting to take my first steps in the ways of the Lord.

I rushed home to Donna and shouted, "Honey, you won't believe this. There really is a Jesus. I got saved and I know it. Jesus lives in me."

She was so afraid. She'd seen me crazy before.

"Honey, you've got to get it. Let's pray," I urged.

"I'm a Catholic, and I go to the Baptist church with you. Isn't that enough?" she asked.

Right after this Donna received Christ and the baptism of the Holy Spirit at a Full Gospel Businessmen's meeting. It was then I said, "If God can touch me, He can touch Monique. Let's pray for her."

We were on the way to an Air Force Hospital. Monique was having four epileptic seizures a day and was taking double the maximum dose of phenobarbitol. We had to go there every month to get an EEG because she had brain damage also. They were trying to control the seizures, but so far they had been unsuccessful.

I said a secret prayer in the truck. We got to the hospital. We had a new doctor because they were going to put Monique on a new program of drugs. The doctor ran the EEG. He said in a very natural way, "It's gone. It's all cleared up—it's gone." He then added, "Quit giving her the medicine."

The other doctors had told Donna and I that she was a drug addict and needed help to take her off her present medicine. "Doctor, are you certain we shouldn't give her drugs?" I questioned.

"I'm certain," was his reply.

From that day she has never had another seizure, or any withdrawals from the medication. I too am free from fear, pills, booze and the other crutches I had clung to for life. My walk with Jesus has removed the hate and bitterness from my heart. Today my family serves Jesus full time—bringing hope and joy to those who have none. Jesus indeed came into this world to set the captives free.

John and his guitar

John, the fisherman

12
ADDING WISDOM TO ZEAL

Donna and I were saved and starting a new life. We were elated over Monique being healed, but there were still trials.

A few days after I got saved and filled with the Holy Ghost, a neighbor who had told me about the Lord before came to talk. I didn't believe him to be a Christian—at least no fruits of a Christian were evident. He said that speaking in tongues was of the devil. Of course, I knew that it could be, because when they started mentioning deliverance this tongue I first spoke was not of God. Afterwards I received a heavenly tongue.

My neighbor was telling me about tongues. I was very ignorant of the Scriptures yet. I'd heard all of the Bible twice on tapes but hadn't studied any of it. He referred me to where the Apostle Paul said "I had rather speak five words with my understanding that by my voice I might teach others also, than ten thousand words in an unknown tongue" (First Corinthians 14:18-19). But he didn't show me where it said, "I thank God I speak with tongues more than ye all," or where Paul said, "I would that ye all spake with tongues." This threw me for a curve. Although I knew that the baptism of the Holy Spirit was not merely speaking in tongues, but that this is what had happened in my life. There was a change in my whole attitude. My whole being was changed.

For a couple of weeks I didn't speak in tongues, but it was always coming to me. It was like words wanting to come out of me. But I thought, I'm not going to say it. Since I didn't know if it was right or wrong, I wasn't going to say it. It didn't seem to make any difference in me at the time. However, I questioned, What good does it do? I didn't have any understanding of how speaking in the tongues edifies one.

One day I started reading what Paul said about it and it all came into view. Why that lying devil, he just deceived me! Right away I started letting the words come out. Praise God, it built me up in the spirit.

The change in my life improved my relationship with Donna a thousand percent. Yet it wasn't long, and I think my zeal without wisdom started to get in the way of some things. I was wanting to go to every meeting any place. We'd just get back from one meeting, and there we were in the car going to another. We couldn't afford it, and some meetings were far away. I wasn't taking care of the farm like I should have.

Even after this wonderful experience of being edified in the spirit I felt so lonesome. I had a compulsion to get rid of anything I enjoyed. I don't feel that way now, but I think it was valid at the time. I enjoyed my pool table. I associated that with drinking, bars, and things like that, so I sold the pool table. To this day I miss it.

We didn't have friends right away, so I'd go see my "friends" in town. They'd be standing around telling dirty jokes and passing around a pint of whiskey. I thought, *Well, they're still my friends.* When I'd come the conversation would change. They wouldn't talk about the same things. They'd seemingly feel uncomfortable around me.

I'd say, "Why don't you guys come up to the house and shoot pool?" (before I sold the pool table). It probably had something to do with me selling the table, too, as long as nobody was going to use it. They wouldn't come up. They did come one time and brought a whole carton full of booze. One guy tried to hold me and pour it down me. I tried to explain that I really didn't want it, that it wasn't just a fad I was going through, that it wasn't that I was trying to be religious—I just didn't want that stuff any more. Later I shared Jesus with him.

One of the men told the rest of the guys, "I think there's really something different about him. Leave him alone. Leave him alone!"

They left and I was kind of upset with God. I knew my life was changed and everything was better, but now I didn't have any friends. I realize now these guys were really not my friends—not like you would consider friends. In a barroom fight, they might have risked their life for me, but only if they were drunk—like we were most of the time. I realize today, they weren't really the kind of friends that I have now.

The only people I had for friends were in the church. We drove to Missouri, over here and over there. We were getting fed spiritually but not in any one particular place. I didn't want to talk about the Bible every second of every day. I didn't want it to dominate my whole life. I still wanted to talk about hunting and fishing. I probably did let the Bible dominate at first, but then it seemed God would be trying to control me, like He wanted me to be His subject (slave), so I stopped that. I just didn't understand the ways of God.

I had planned to go to Bill's but I told Donna, "I feel like going and getting drunk. I don't want to get drunk. I just want somebody to be my friend. I've got to have friends." We prayed that night.

I had already planned to get drunk the next day, but three different families that we didn't know before came by to visit. We'd met them at the churches we'd been visiting. So we made new friends.

Before I knew God I had tried to get into the Masons. Being a drunkard, I couldn't get into that organization. So after I was saved and filled with the Holy Ghost, they sent a representative to the house to check me out. He was impressed because all I wanted to talk about was Jesus. They would have had to get a special waiver to get me in the Masons because I couldn't give the certain right-hand handshake.

I had a real strong check in my spirit about becoming a Mason. Yet, I think my pride overrode it because I'd wanted to for so long and couldn't. Now that I could I felt I shouldn't. I talked to a Baptist preacher about it. I asked, "What does this mean that you should not take an oath?"

"All that means is if you take the oath, you are supposed to keep it." Then he added, "I'm a Mason."

So I went through riding the goat and joined the Masons. One meeting, and just once through the ritual was enough for me to know that it didn't have anything to do with Jesus. I found that before I was there I wasn't good enough to get in. However, after I got in I found the place was full of drunks. But after you are in—you are in. You can do anything after you are in. Boy, that hit me like a time bomb—the death oath and the whole bit.

Then they started taking me out for my second degree, teaching me. They stuck themselves out on a limb to get special permission to get me in. I said, "You guys, I don't really want to." I didn't know how to tell them that I didn't want to be a Mason after I'd become one. Finally I said, "You guys, I just have a check in my spirit about it right now. I don't want to go through any more of the training." I didn't see a whole lot of sin there, but I didn't see anything of Jesus there. "Maybe this is all right for you guys, but it's more important for me to preach."

"This is like church," they said.

Well, of course, it wasn't like the churches that I was going to and feeling the presence of God.

Then Donna and I started taking in foster kids. By now we had bought a large farm and moved into a condemned house in town, while we were building a new house on the farm. The condemned house was in terrible condition. While there I began donating three days a week at a Baptist boy's ranch. I was helping them to do anything—castrating the hogs, working with the boys, just anything.

One of the boys at the ranch was demon-possessed. So I told some people, "That boy is demon-possessed."

Some said, "There's nothing we can do about it." Others said, "Yes, we know, but we can't do anything about it here in this particular Baptist facility."

I went home, and apparently the boy was on my mind. I prayed much about it. One day the Lord showed me in a vision that I was going to get Jimmy S., and that he would be coming home with me. I tried to laugh it off and said, "There's no way. I'm not a licensed foster parent. I've never applied. I'm not interested in it, and he's got a home there."

The Ranch was almost second to reform school. They couldn't get out of there, and they could be pretty rough with them if they didn't go along with the program. Jimmy had been in reform school and had twelve federal convictions against him already. At the age of twelve years he had done about everything.

I went to Doc's house and there were some other people there who asked, "Brother John, would you consider taking Jimmy home with you?"

I questioned, "Why? Why do you want me to take him?"

"Because we can't do anything with him. He's been to reform school. He's been to jail and to a mental institution. We cannot keep him here because he disrupts everything. Would you take him because if you don't we're sending him back to reform school."

"Yes, I'll take him."

After we were saved, maybe six months, I remember that I was afraid of deliverance because I knew it was real. I knew what had happened to me, and I was scared to death of demons. I didn't want to talk about it. I didn't want to joke about it. I didn't want anything to do with deliverance. But when Jimmy came to live with us I started reading everything I could on it, and going through everything in the Scriptures on it. I found in Mark that over a third of Jesus' ministry was in deliverance, but I was still afraid of it. This was pretty heavy business we're talking about. I didn't, like some charismatics, take it lightly. I knew that I at one time was full of devils.

Jimmy came to live with us. He kept a bottle of gasoline hid all over the place and sniffed it. He had terrible migraine headaches, but yet he always sniffed this gasoline. He would take off his clothes and run around the block with a torch in his hand. He was just crazy. I had to nail shut the back door of the condemned home to keep him from slipping out at night. I was always taking cigarettes out of his pockets. He swore somebody at school would stuff them in there—he didn't know where they came from. It was one lie after another. I was always at the school with him because he was in trouble.

One day a lady ran him into the house. He had called her "sparkplug." Apparently somebody had done something to this lady at one time with a sparkplug that wasn't very nice. Jimmy didn't know what it was, but he'd go by the house and holler, "Hey, sparkplug." She ran right into my house to get him. The kid was in all kinds of trouble.

He tried to fight me in the front yard. I had told him to do something. He was a thirteen-year-old, skinny little kid with big black circles under his eyes, with kinky-like blond hair. He was screaming and cursing me. As the devil would have it, all the neighbors were standing out on their front porches, watching me.

The only thing I could do was pick him up and slam him up against the house, and hold him there while he was trying to fight me. I saw the neighbors looking at me as I picked him up and threw him into the back room of the house. I didn't know what to do.

We had a big poster picture of Jesus, and I dropped down on my knees and began to cry out to God: "God, send a deliverance minister. Help me with this boy. God, help me!"

The Lord spoke to me saying, "I'm the minister. I'm the deliverer." He then said for me to go to Jim and lay hands on him. I was really afraid to do that, but I did.

I went in there and said, "In the name of Jesus, devil, come out of him." Immediately he began vomiting slime all over the room. I was praising the Lord and He said, "It's not done yet."

"What do you mean it's not done? Look what happened."

Again He said, "It's not done yet."

I laid hands on him again. As soon as I did he began to vomit again. I prayed for him two or three times like that. Afterwards I went through the same thing with him that I'd been through and asked, "Do you feel empty? Do you feel all cleaned out? How would you like to fill up that emptiness?" I led him to the Lord, and then he got the Holy Spirit. We had Jimmy for about three years.

He was always causing us problems. He didn't really want to serve the Lord with his whole heart, but we did see God deliver him from epileptic seizures and migraines. About two months ago I went to visit Jimmy in the Benton prison. I've visited several of "my boys" in prison. I know the seed of the Gospel is planted. Sometimes I don't hear from them for two, three or four years, but they always come back to me and say, "John, you never lied to me." Their whole life they'd been lied to by the Welfare, by the Police Department, and their parents.

If their parents said, "If you do thus and so, I'm going to spank you." Their parents didn't spank them. They'd just curse or kick them. In the Police Department they'd tell them when they'd come to our house, "You don't have to do anything at Brother John's." They'd say, "You can have long hair there." They lied to them. I had set orders that we wouldn't take any foster kids unless they had their hair cut.

When they'd come to my house I'd say, "We don't lie here. If I tell you I'm going to spank you if you do thus and thus, I'll spank you. If I tell you we'll go fishing, I don't care if it's raining, we'll go fishing," and that's what we did for three or four years. We had sixteen kids all together. That's how we got into deliverance.

Back in 1978 after we had the big farm, we had all these foster kids at different times, and the Lord slowly moved them out. There were trials and problems that we went through. There would always be fighting. One time one of them would have beat up Donna if I hadn't backed him off. We really went through trials with them. The only place Donna could go and really pray or be alone was in the bathroom.

One of the hardest things for Donna, after I became a Christian, was that at first I was still like I was when I was having problems. I'd slam the door, or come up to her and say, "I'd like to punch you," but I didn't. I was still very impulsive and impatient. I had changed in almost all other ways. The Lord had delivered me from all the things I had done except in this one area. So when I said, "We're going to Mexico," I sold the big farm and went to do missionary work, way down by the Guatemala border.

Of course, that meant Donna washing our clothes on a cement rub board and 110 degree weather. First of all, it was a cultural shock for her. That took a while to get over. One day she was washing clothes on a washer some missionaries had bought the Mexicans. They had never used it because they didn't know how. Pauline, the wife of another couple who had come with us, said, "I know how." Donna had never used a wringer-type washer.

We were using it and Monique and Donna were helping her wash. She got tired so went back to her van. Monique and Donna were finishing up. Monique, who was seven years old, found that she could put the clothes through the wringer which Donna had been washing. She said, "Yes, but be very careful because your hand could get in there and it could take your whole arm all the way up."

"Oh, yes," she promised, "I will be careful." Donna had gone to hang up the clothes on the line and heard her screaming, "Mama, help me! Help me!"

She turned around and there her little hand was in the wringer. She was pulling with her other hand to pull her hand out, and screaming, "Mama, help me! Help me!" She didn't know what to do. She just stood there and couldn't think or do anything. What a feeling to just be so helpless—to know that there is nothing you can do and here your little child is screaming, "Mama, help me!"

Pauline's son, Tim, was there. Donna looked at him and he just stood in shock. She looked at the Mexicans and they just stood there. Everybody was like in shock. Then she started screaming at the top of her lungs for me. I was on the other side of the little church, about seventy feet away, sitting in a van. I heard the screaming and thought it was Mexicans going by and hollering.

Then it was like the Lord impressed her to unplug the machine. This stopped Monique's hand from going through, but there she was with her hand stuck in the wringer. Her thumb didn't go in and was pulled back almost to her wrist. She was still screaming, "Mama, can't you get me out of this thing?" This was a Mexican-type washing machine and it had no quick release on it. It was tightened down with a wrench on top. Donna had it unplugged and tried to pry it apart with her hands, but wasn't strong enough. Since she couldn't do anything she ran to the van where I was.

People from across the street started following me, I realized then it was Donna screaming. I'd been listening to the screams—it seemed like twenty seconds—and thought it was a little kid. All of a sudden I see it's my wife. What's going on? I began screaming in tongues at the top of my lungs. I ran toward the screams and saw Monique about ready to faint. Her hand was black and looked mangled, and the thumb was pulled back to the wrist. Donna couldn't even look.

A bunch of Mexicans followed me there and they were all standing around. I think I just stuck my hook in the rollers. We got the thing pried open and got Monique's hand out. I took her hand and said, "Hand, I command you in the name of Jesus Christ of Nazareth, be made whole." Right in front of everybody God healed her. We know it's healed because she's playing the piano with it now.

Since then we have ministered in many places in Mexico. We built and painted a church in Nuevo Larado, Mexico. We also ministered ten months in La Loma Prison in Nuevo Larado. We have seen the Lord move in a mighty way there, and led twenty-one persons from El Salvador to the Lord one day. They were trying to escape the conflict in their own country when the Mexican police picked them up and put them in prison.

We left that work there when a Mexican lawyer told me not to go back to the prison. He heard there was a plan to keep me there. They now have Christians in the prison to carry on the work. I had prayed, <u>Lord, show me what You want.</u> He showed me the Scripture where it said when they persecute you in one city to flee to the next. It broke my heart that I was not free to go back to the prison.

We have been ministering in and out of Haiti, where we have built churches and orphanages. We also travel throughout the States doing the work of an evangelist.

John & Festival singing at Washington, DC in front of a crowd of 40,000 at the dedication of the Vietnam Memorial Wall and Statue.

13
CURSE OR BLESSING?

Now that you've read my testimony and have an idea of where I've been, and some of the things I've done, I hope that through reading this you will begin to understand the longsuffering and mercy our Lord had for me and HAS FOR YOU.

I did not write this book because I am proud of my old life. Neither did I write it to become famous, or to make a fast buck. I wrote the book because of the Holy Spirit dealing with my heart. There are a lot of you guys that have similar problems and *I KNOW the answer*.

It was very painful for me, going back over all the details of my life and exposing myself before you. But the Lord put me together with Cliff Dudley, and without his help this book would never have gotten written. He gave me love and encouragement as we spent many long hours reliving and writing about my past.

I know there are many of you who have your head screwed on backwards. Your life is filled with booze, drugs, or else you just hide your feelings and pretend everything is all right. If it is all right, why do you feel guilty? Why do you hate yourself? Why aren't you happy with your wife and kids? Why do you sometimes get knots of hate in the pit of your stomach? Why do you say in your heart nobody understands, nobody cares?

Then there are those who think we are sissies because we have problems. You may claim you have it all together. I praise God if you do. But I've read too many newspaper clippings, seen too many TV shows talking about Vietnam vets committing suicide, robbing stores, getting killed in car wrecks. I quote from *DAV*, January 1980:

STARTLING STATISTICS: 1) Statistics gathered three years ago indicate that the suicide rate among Vietnam veterans is of higher percentage than among the general population. John P. Wilson, Ph.D., who conducted the "Forgotten Warrior" research project for the DAV, believes the suicide rate among Vietnam veterans has now climbed to a percentage higher than the national average. 2) Of those veterans who were married before going to Vietnam, 38% were divorced within six months after returning from Southeast Asia. 3) Between 40-60% of the veterans of the Vietnam War have persistent problems with emotional adjustment. 4) The number of

Vietnam veterans hospitalized for alcoholism or drinking problems has more than doubled in the past seven years.

You will note that these statistics are old, but I know that as a whole, the problems are not getting better but worse.

To you that have problems, and to you who think you don't have any problems, I have the answer. It's a sellout to Jesus Christ. Some may say you have tried religion. I'm not talking about religion. I'm talking about a personal experience with Jesus Christ, the author and finisher of our faith.

When I went through jump school at Fort Benning, Georgia, it took every fiber of my being to get through it, and it was the same with some of the training you took. If you would put half that much effort into seeking the Lord—I promise He will meet you. "Ask, and it shall be given you; seek, and you shall find; and to him that knocks it shall be opened." "All things work together for good to them that love God and are called according to his purpose."

I'm beginning to understand how God loved me so much He allowed me to go to Vietnam and to see and do all the terrible things I did and saw because He knew this is what it would take to break me and cause me to repent and serve Him. "For whom he did foreknow, he also did predestinate to be conformed to the image of his Son" (Romans 8:29). Jesus knew I would eventually serve Him. I praise Him for not letting me die out there and to go to hell, and for not taking His hand of protection off of me.

My rebelliousness reminds me a little of my oldest son John. The other day I was rolling out some barbed wire to put up a fence. John, who is 9, asked if he could roll it out. "No," I said, "you will get scratched up." He had no gloves on. He continued to persist: "No, I won't. No, I won't."

"Yes, you will," I said. Finally I realized he needed a lesson—he would never believe me otherwise. So I let him roll out the wire. Well, he got his hands all scratched up. Now maybe next time I tell him something he will believe me. I didn't allow him to get scratched up because I don't love him. He persisted on having his own way.

And so it is with the Lord. He has a perfect plan for your life. But until you decide to do it His way you are going to get scratched up. Listen for that still small voice beckoning you to accept Him and serve Him. Jesus is the *ONLY* answer.

Vietnam—was it a curse or a blessing? A little of both.

If you would like to contact John Steer you may write to:

John Steer
HC 31, Box 4
Charlotte, AR 72522